WHAT'S NEXT?

Rachel Curtis Gravesen

HealthCap and the Art of Venture Capital

PAINTINGS BY JESPER WALDERSTEN

MAX STRÖM

Contents

Preface

WHEN WRITING THIS in early 2022, the world has just experienced two true *anni horribiles*, caused by the virus SARS-COV-2, only to be thrown into a devastating war in Europe, causing further human suffering and damage to society. Lives have been wasted, businesses ruined, and public health systems challenged. This book has been written under the dire conditions of travel bans, lockdowns, and other limitations to human interaction. The author, Rachel Curtis Gravesen, has not been able to meet physically with most of the people interviewed in the book, but, despite this, she managed to get very close to us and our stakeholders.

The use of new technologies has provided a creative platform where digital interaction has made possible the assemblance of a story that started already before the internet became an everyday commodity. This pays tribute to the theme of the book, namely how new discovery and subsequent development of useful technology can be of great help to man and mankind. It is also of interest to remember the pivotal role that venture capital played in supporting the development of the internet and the subsequent explosion in the way it is used in our daily lives.

The emergence of a myriad of web-based technology companies, including household names such as Apple, Compaq, Google, and Amazon, etc., have depended on or have been accelerated by the financial support and insightful backing from venture capital. Although a relatively small geographical area, San Francisco Bay became an epicentre of innovation where close relationships based on both formal and informal interaction developed between the region's engineers, scientists, universities, government, and venture capitalists, allowing for the rapid diffusion of technologies, skills, and know-how. Repeat entrepreneurs and scientists continued to innovate and found new ventures, and successful venture capitalists could raise more funds to finance novel endeavours. This highlights the inherent nature of venture capital, namely the combination of openness and collaboration, but also healthy competition.

HealthCap is headquartered in Stockholm, Sweden, a small country with a strong pedigree in life sciences and a track record of export-dependent industries and an open economy. From the outset we decided not to confine ourselves to the geographic boundaries of Scandinavia, but to look at life sciences as the truly global business it is. We argued that a medical problem is the same in Europe as it is in the United States or anywhere in the world, and the solutions to these problems are therefore universal. We also argued that in order to profitably develop new therapeutic products, you need to take a global approach to a product's market. This meant that every portfolio company of ours should in parallel develop, or at least have a plan for development of, its product for approval in many geographies. It also meant that we were eager to invest in companies and ideas in other geographies than Scandinavia.

The discussions with our investors, our limited partners, were long and intense. One line of argument was that we should focus on our home turf because it would be hard to manage overseas investments in a diligent way. Another that we would always be second to the best opportunities. We stood our ground, which probably turned out to be an important success factor for HealthCap. We were thus able to start companies in many countries based on brilliant ideas brought to us by many sources, most notably our informal network of "HealthChaps". This approach does not come easy, and it demands an intellectual and physical presence on many occasions such as participation in international scientific conferences, trade gatherings, etc., to earn respect and acumen in the global life science community and to become a trustworthy partner to entrepreneurs and fellow investors far from home. Looking back at our first 25 years, I would like to think that we have made a broad and important impact. To date, HealthCap has invested in 126 ventures and taken 46 companies public on fourteen different stock exchanges in almost as many countries. The accumulated market capitalization of these companies now exceeds EUR 50 billion and more than 50,000 jobs have been created, directly and indirectly.

Our international approach also meant that we could learn a lot from experienced peers, and over the years, exceptional relationships have developed with many of the world's most knowledgeable venture capital organisations and life science specialist investors. We have been welcomed into this esteemed community, I believe because we bring value and knowledge to the party, and in the United States it certainly helps that we have a different perspective and understanding of the European regulatory system and markets.

These first 25 years we have resisted the temptation to open a physical office in the United States, the world's greatest melting pot for life science innovation. Instead, we have guarded our European legacy and argued the value of keeping our partner team in one spot, in fact one big room, where ideas and problems immediately can be bounced around, exceeded the value of having offices in several countries.

When it comes to SARS-COV-2 and COVID-19, it might be too early to claim victory over the disease, but some interesting and important conclusions can be drawn already.

The vaccines that became game-changers were initially developed by small innovative companies and universities. Big pharma was an important partner in this endeavour, putting the spotlight on collaboration as state-of-the-art in life sciences. The venture capital community was part of the solution by backing the young companies that developed the novel technologies which became useful vaccines. Moderna and BioNTech pushed the limits for what was perceived as possible when introducing the concept of injecting messenger-RNA as a blueprint for the desired antigens that trigger the body's immune response to the virus. Without daring support from early venture investors, these technologies would not have been developed.

Oxford university pursued a semi-novel path by making use of a harmless virus to carry the blueprint into the body. This technology benefits from the numerous endeavours utilizing various virus vectors for delivering genetic code to the body, the very back-bone of modern gene therapy. This therapeutic area has been backed and built by venture capital and big pharma in tandem. HealthCap has, as well as many other venture capital firms, made several investments in the area over the years and supported efforts such as Targovax, Ultragenyx, GenSight, Vivet, and Carisma, and more recently in our eighth venture fund, Mahzi, and Aro.

Just as technological conquests provided a launchpad for the emerging computer and internet industries, the currently remarkable ongoing evolution of biological sciences is providing us with an in-depth understanding of the underlying molecular mechanisms of disease. Our time can fairly be described as a golden age for life sciences, as we now at an increasing pace gain insights on novel and more precise ways to treat disease by targeting the root causes. For example, today we understand that cancer is not one disease but many different diseases, each with its own molecular cause, each which should be therapeutically approached accordingly with a precision medicine mindset. By treating the right patient with the right medicine higher efficacy is gained, side-effects can be reduced, and development time of new pharmaceuticals can be shortened.

HealthChaps is our name for the informal network of exceptional individuals that we have had the opportunity to collaborate or interact closely with over the years. They are scientists, industry leaders, regulators, lawyers, former board members or management of portfolio companies. We meet an enormous flow of ideas and investment proposals that can sometimes be overwhelming, but opportunities stemming from HealthChaps stand out with respect to their quality and uniqueness. We have always tried to follow the credo "Work hard and be nice to people". Our many HealthChaps serve as a tribute to this approach.

In general, venture capital is a tough but very collaborative business. It contains, of course, elements of risk-taking, but the most significant characteristics of venture investing are those of a mutual journey together with individuals and organisations that each participate valuably and contribute to reaching a successful outcome. Just as in the emergence of Silicon Valley, syndication is still a key element in a winning venture. This is the practice of several venture capital firms joining forces in an effort to create a thriving company. No doubt, there is competition between venture capital firms, but we benefit from each other's perspectives.

This book tells our story from start-up to today's professional investment organisation. It is one of ups and downs, the greater need for optimism than pessimism, and extraordinary contributions from individuals and teams. It is one of failed investments and successes, but since the balance is on the positive side, we have been given the means to continue *our* venture. On this journey, millions of patients with severe illness have been helped by the 30 pharmaceutical products and more than 50 medtech products that have been brought to market by our companies, while tens of thousands of jobs have been created. So, thanks to the joint efforts of our supportive investors, passionate HealthChaps, team members and co-travellers, the world might have become a slightly better place. Wishing you an interesting read.

Björn Odlander

A Walk in the Park?

THE TWO MEN sitting on the same bench in a park in central Stockholm every day could, from a distance, easily have been mistaken for vagrants. On closer look, though, they were suit-clad businessmen, doing their daily work on mobile phones.

The two men, Björn Odlander and Peder Fredrikson, had been colleagues at a Swedish investment bank but had just taken a leap of faith and resigned so that they could pursue their dream – investing in innovative ideas that had the potential to become healthcare products that would help patients by addressing unmet medical needs.

It might sound like the start of a fairytale, but it was there, sitting on that park bench in Humlegården, that officeless Odlander and Fredrikson started to work on their shared vision and ambition to build a company. That company was HealthCap, a venture capital business where funding from investors could be put to work to support and develop innovative ideas coming from the life science sector. Twenty-five years on, HealthCap has raised over EUR 1.2 billion for investment in the life science industry, backed and built over 125 companies and seen more than 30 pharmaceutical products and more than 50 med-tech products approved for use in the healthcare sector.

> "We had a clear idea from day one on what we felt we could achieve," Odlander says, looking out from HealthCap's current head office next to the very park where it all started.

Founded in 1996, the Swedish internationally focused venture capital firm HealthCap has taken the journey that it expects its own portfolio companies to make: from being a start-up without an office space to fighting to survive during a couple of global financial downturns before growing into the more mature business of today, where the most recent venture fund, HealthCap VIII, exceeded target levels to reach a total of over EUR 230 million. As was the case with funds HealthCap I to VII, the capital in HealthCap VIII will be invested in scientific innovations for unmet medical needs – turning science into medicines or products for people who need them.

Looking at it from the backdrop of today's sophisticated global financial sector, it seems strange to think that venture capital was a new concept in Europe back in the 1990s. Venture capital, where investors provide early-stage funding for start-ups or young businesses that show potential for long-term growth, had emerged in the US in the 1960s and 1970s, mainly as a way of funding early technology companies in Silicon Valley. Europe, however, was still reliant on bank financing or so-called private equity, where buy-out funds often invested in more mature companies operating in traditional industries, rather than in high-risk innovations, where they created value by ironing out inefficiencies so that businesses became more profitable. Venture capital is more likely to be invested in promising private companies with a high growth potential – often new ideas that are creating new or disrupting established markets – and relies almost exclusively on equity as the vehicle for financing.

Europe, and not least Sweden, was – and still is – home to a wealth of scientific expertise. HealthCap's founders Odlander and Fredrikson believed there was a need for investor support to take some of these high-risk but potentially game-changing scientific innovations out of academia and into the commercial landscape. They both understood that turning scientific innovation into medicines and medical devices that might ultimately help patients was expensive and needed large amounts of funding. They also both understood that most of these ideas would not make it as far as the market.

Drug development is a long-term game, with a rule of thumb that for every 100 projects started in a lab, only one will be commercialised. Private equity investors were often wary of funding start-ups due to the long and often twisting journey involved in developing new therapeutics and devices from innovative idea into a product that might eventually be commercialised and deliver returns.

With strict ethical and developmental regulations covering the life science industry, it was also often challenging for private equity investors, who may not have a medical or scientific background, to know which ideas to back. How could they navigate the many ideas and hypotheses from innovators, selecting which projects could end as much-needed products for patients? The potential rewards from picking a winner could be high, but there was also a great risk of failure.

Odlander and Fredrikson realised they had the skill set to identify potential winners and explain to investors why certain innovations were exciting opportunities. Odlander, a qualified Doctor of Medicine (MD) and former research scientist at Stockholm's Karolinska Institutet, understood the financial world, having become a top-rated healthcare equity research analyst at ASEA Brown Boveri's (ABB) investment bank Aros Securities in the 1990s. Fredrikson had enjoyed a long and successful career in the global financial sector working in American investment banks, including Bank of America and Morgan Stanley.

Both also believed that a global perspective in life science was imperative. People with unmet medical needs and the innovative ideas designed to meet those needs were not confined to particular countries or regions but could be found all over the world. With Odlander and Fredrikson's complimentary skills, energy and shared global vision, HealthCap – a venture capital firm based in Sweden with a life science focus – was born.

All his life, Odlander has been driven by a keen sense of curiosity. As well as an interest in science, he is enthusiastic about literature, art and architecture – and has developed a passion for food and wine. Odlander began his professional career in the world of academia, as a research student in the labs of Nobel Laureate Bengt Samuelsson, where he gained his PhD in Physiological Chemistry of Inflammation. Speaking about his time in the lab, HealthCap co-founder Odlander remembers:

> "Bengt Samuelsson is an eminent scientist, and I was thrilled to be working in his lab. What became clear was that he also had a strong belief in the innovation philosophy that without new technologies there is no new discovery. I realised the need for funding to ensure new discoveries also led to new innovations."

Although enjoying the academic world of scientific research, Odlander was intrigued about the idea of combining his analytical skills and understanding of biochemistry within the world of finance. He therefore took a leap into the unknown and joined the investment bank ABB Aros Securities, later becoming head of Health Care Equity Research. He was voted best pharmaceutical analyst four years in a row, from 1993 to 1996, by the leading Swedish business journal *Affärsvärlden*. It was at Aros

Securities he met his soon-to-be co-founder Fredrikson and the idea for HealthCap was born. In 1996, they took a deep breath and made the decision to leave Aros to start out on their own.

Fredrikson believed investors derived comfort from his and Odlander's background: "Even though we had been working together in the investment bank Aros for some years, neither Björn nor I had a record as successful investors per se, but the institutions were prepared to accept Björn's incredible reputation as a top-rated analyst and my international investment banking background credentials, so they trusted our ability to run the VC in a professional way."

Odlander continues:

"It was quite scary to think about untying the moorings and sailing away on our own, leaving the secure framework of the investment bank. We had no assurance that institutions would find HealthCap attractive enough, and although Peder and I had been successful within Aros Securities, we were now a two-man band. However, we never doubted the need for a venture capital fund in life science based in Scandinavia, and we were convinced it offered a great opportunity."

So, in May 1996 both men quit lucrative, secure careers in banking and, once the park bench became too impractical, set up in borrowed office space on Birger Jarlsgatan in Stockholm, with desks created out of stacked cardboard boxes that had been left by the previous tenant and supportive friends, AMCO Capital. In true start-up style, they purchased mobile phones on special offer at a local shopping centre:

"But with numbers in sequence like a real company," Odlander proudly remembers with a smile. Shortly afterwards the partners were joined by employee number three – Lena Porin – who took the risk of joining the start-up to help organise the administration side of the business. Looking back at her long tenure with HealthCap, Lena, who is now known by her married name Olby, says:

"I must admit that I felt brave when joining HealthCap 25 years ago – coming from a safe and interesting job with ABB Financial Services." Olby continues: "It's been such an honour to be part of this successful journey. It's motivating to see how HealthCap's support helps our portfolio companies pursue their goal of creating new inventions and treatments that could benefit so many patients."

In the spring of 1996, Odlander and Fredrikson spent hours persuading investors to believe in their idea and invest in their first fund. Several well-respected leaders lent key support to the two partners. Legal advisor Ulf Söderholm and his team put together state-of-the-art contracts to ensure that HealthCap's business met the highest institutional requirements. This framework was checked and endorsed by supportive prospective lead investors Thomas Halvorsen, from the Swedish state's Fourth National Pension Fund (Fjärde AP-fonden, or Fourth AP fund), and Per Johan Björnstedt, at the life insurance company Skandia. At Handelsbanken, Kjell Ormegard, Head of Investment Banking, ensured a level of credibility for the young start-up by supporting the business in various ways – not least by serving as placement agent and putting Handelsbanken's logo on the front of HealthCap's investment memorandum for the prospective fund.

Odlander and Fredrikson also had a very clear idea of the kind of culture they wanted to create at the company. As a small company, where each person plays an important role, new team members were chosen because of their personalities as well as their skill sets. So, the group was soon expanded with Dr Magnus Persson, a former research colleague of Odlander's from the Karolinska Institutet. Odlander remembers:

> "Our institutional backers identified that we needed to broaden our organisation to be more resilient. People worried about what would happen if, typically, I were to be run over by a bus, hit by a falling brick or many other imaginative ways that would end my earthly life." He continues: "Magnus was an ideal partner to add to our small group, based on his strong medical and academic pedigree, and easy-going personality."

Later that year, as the first snow fell at the beginning of winter, the small team's tenacity and strong reputations in the life science and banking sectors paid off. Cornerstone investors, in the shape of the Fourth AP fund and Skandia, committed to HealthCap I. Soon after, other key investors followed – Astra, Pharmacia & Upjohn, Länsförsäkringar, the Knut and Alice Wallenberg Foundation and Handelsbanken all committed to investing in the fund. The company had not only hit the ground running but was now also gaining speed.

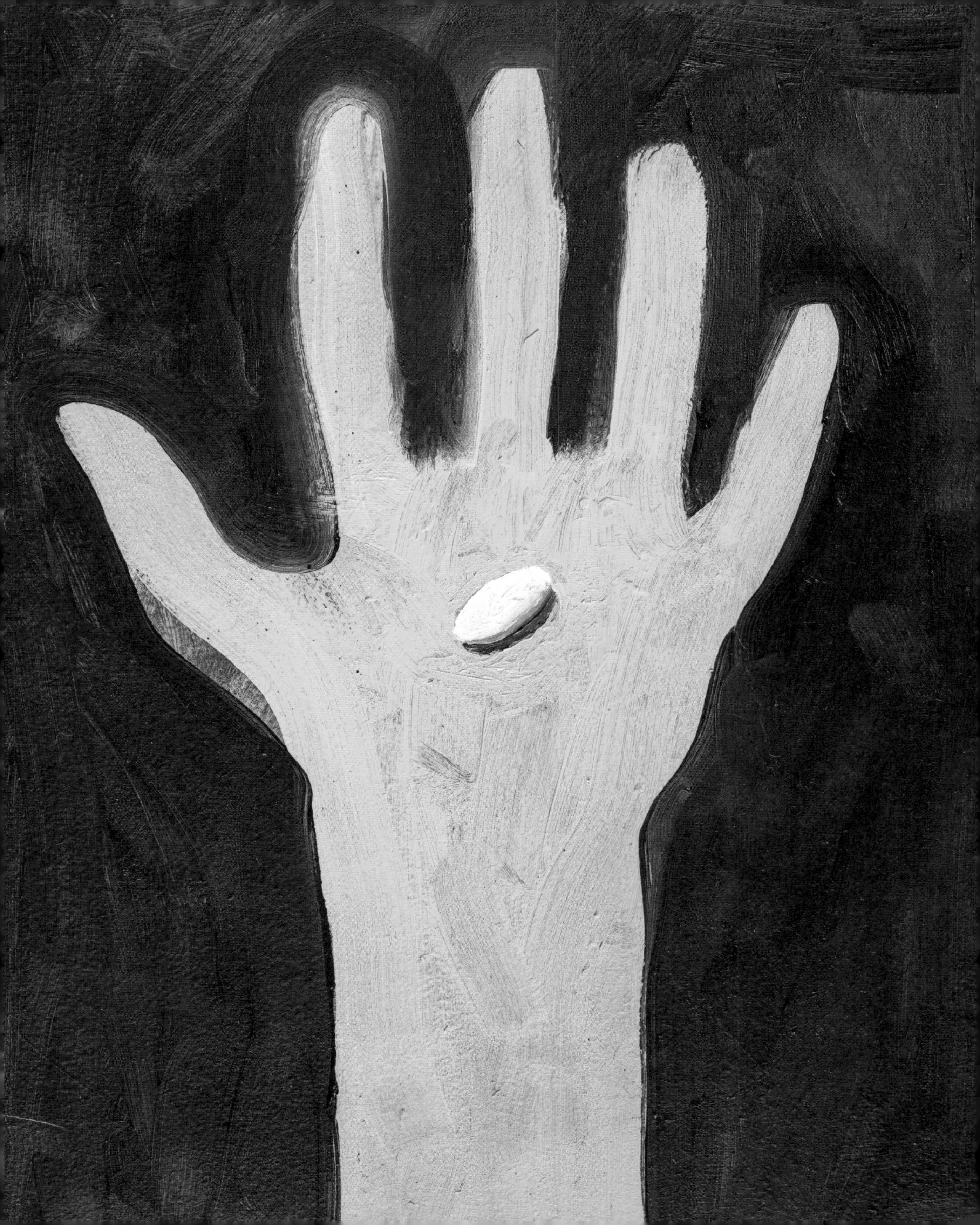

Venture Capital Saves Lives

WHAT IS A venture capitalist (or VC, as they are known for short)? Broadly speaking, a VC is a private equity investor that provides funding and know-how to companies with high growth potential in exchange for an equity stake. In the life science sector this often translates into investment in innovative ideas that can end as medicines or other products to treat disease.

When Björn Odlander and Peder Fredrikson started HealthCap, the financial landscape looked very different.

> "Back in the 90s, there was no real venture capital model in Sweden, so we had to invent it when starting HealthCap," explains Odlander. "Peder and I had enjoyed success building a healthcare franchise in Aros Securities and we were convinced that with our combined expertise we would be able to create a strong team with a venture fund to support innovation in the life science sector, while creating returns for investors."

As many of HealthCap's portfolio companies discover, it is sometimes hard to persuade people to support innovations that challenge current thinking. Many traditional Swedish investors had been burnt when an early effort by some of the large cap Swedish companies and institutions to invest in higher-risk start-ups did not produce the expected positive results. Odlander and Fredrikson wanted to change all that, and in the first 25 years, HealthCap has built a track record of funding 126 companies, 12 of which became so-called unicorns and 46 companies became listed on the public markets. From this support, 30 drugs and more than 50 healthtech products have been approved. Fredrikson continues:

"In the early days in the 80s, the large institutions and corporations in Sweden tried to enter venture capitalism by starting a fund. It didn't work well at all, so there was resistance to investing in such funds when we started out."

But there were a few individuals who shared Odlander and Fredrikson's views. Fredrikson: "There were pockets of people who understood that this type of funding was really needed, so we did manage to raise HealthCap I and HealthCap II virtually back to back, but I wouldn't say it was easy."

In Fredrikson's view, HealthCap has impacted the life science landscape in Sweden and globally, in both investment and knowledge terms. The investment pool has grown so that it is easier to fund good, innovative ideas, enabling the life science sector in the Nordic region to flourish. Having backing from a domestic venture capitalist with a good international reputation lends credibility and comfort for global investors. HealthCap's reputation and knowledge base has also led to a broader understanding of the benefits of venture capitalism in the region. "We have had an important role as a catalyst for other venture capital funds established in the Nordic area, not just those with a life science focus but also for venture capitalists in other sectors."

Fredrikson is convinced that life science funding via venture capital is essential: "Particularly as governmental support is difficult to attract with timelines on return of investment of maybe ten years or more. We have helped to impact the landscape by encouraging other forms of investment, so Sweden in particular has enjoyed billions and billions of kronor of funding support in the life science industry."

Early on in HealthCap's lifetime, Odlander understood the importance of getting good advice and controlling your own destiny: "Although we got offers to sell part of the business, our advisors and our belief in our skills and experience made us keen to stay independent."

Odlander continues:

"We had some wonderful and outstanding people supporting us from the start. These individuals became the core in what we still see as one of our key strengths – HealthChaps, our name for the network of individuals with whom we work and interact closely, and we prize them as dearly today as we did at the start."

Odlander sees the value of getting good advice when starting out, and a key focus for the HealthCap team is to provide this kind of strategic support to portfolio companies.

Two of the most important advisors from the start of the HealthCap journey were Professor Bengt Samuelsson, the 1982 Nobel Laureate in Physiology or Medicine, and the late Frank Caufield, a legend in the venture capital world and former partner in the renowned American venture capital firm Kleiner Perkins Caufield & Byers. Fredrikson and Odlander were convinced that having access to advice from doyens in areas relevant for life science venture investing not only provided name recognition, but – more importantly – would also lead to better business decisions.

Caufield provided some realistic thoughts on the common challenges that could occur in starting a venture capital fund. As Fredrikson recalls:

> "It is difficult to be a first-time fund raiser. In June 1996 when we started out, we were quite optimistic, but our advisor Frank Caufield predicted it would snow before we raised funds. I took the unofficial bet that I believed we could close before snowfall came. Some five months later, on 29 November when we were walking to the bank for the official close of HealthCap I, it started snowing. So, I lost the bet! But I have to say, I was very pleased we had achieved raising the money for the first fund."

An Investor's Gut Instinct

HAVING A GOOD idea doesn't always lead to a successful business. Having the right people running the business and following a focused strategy often does. Life science investments carry a certain level of risk, but also have a high reward profile. However, to pick potential winners can be tricky, requiring an understanding of the science behind an innovation as well as having the business acumen to develop an idea and grow a company so that the idea becomes a viable product.

In 1996, Thomas Halvorsen was a seasoned pension fund manager running the Fourth AP fund (which today is worth over SEK 400 billion or around EUR 39 billion). Halvorsen was approached by HealthCap's founders Björn Odlander and Peder Fredrikson. They were starting their first venture capital fund independently, without the backing of a large sponsor, having left their steady jobs at ABB Aros Securities.

Halvorsen knew that investing in life science innovations was high risk and that some of his counterparts in the investment community would be cautious about investing in a fund targeted at this sector. But he also saw the strength of the pair's skill sets in research, medicine, banking and business, as well as their energy and enthusiasm. He liked the idea of a venture capital fund – HealthCap I – that would provide funding for life science innovations that could lead to benefits for patients. Halvorsen also felt this long-term focus for creating value fitted with the Fourth AP fund's mandate to invest its capital to gain high returns over a longer horizon.

Despite the high-risk element, Halvorsen was attracted to HealthCap's vision, and had confidence that Odlander and Fredrikson had experience that might help them balance risk as much as possible to create long-term value. Halvorsen recalls: "Björn and Peder had very different personalities with clear and complimentary skill sets, and together they were very strong."

Halvorsen recognised the broad spectrum of knowledge across the life science sector and the world of business that Odlander and Fredrikson brought to the table: experience and skills that could help start-ups and scientists shape and define a strategy to develop innovations into viable assets.

In the spring of 1996 Halvorsen, together with his deputy Björn Franzon, invited Odlander and Fredrikson to lunch at the plush restaurant Operakällaren in central Stockholm. He had decided that the Fourth AP fund would be a cornerstone investor in the first HealthCap fund, HealthCap I. Odlander and Fredrikson could not have been more pleased; they knew that this commitment would reassure other potential investors and business partners and open the way for them to raise the fund. HealthCap I was closed some five months later, on 29 November 1996.

Although Halvorsen believed firmly in the value of a venture capital fund in Sweden, and he was impressed with Odlander and Fredrikson's innovative spirit, he was also very aware of the risks with this type of venture. At lunch he warned them of the challenges to come that might dent their motivation: "It was a very nice restaurant with really good food. I told them to make sure they ate a good lunch during our meeting – as they might be hungry in the near future."

In Halvorsen's view, Odlander and Fredrikson created the right base for HealthCap to deliver on bringing life science innovations to the next level. He believed in their ability to create employment, encourage innovation and develop potential breakthrough therapies and devices for patients who needed them. "What I have learnt is that what really matters is management, and Peder and Björn complemented each other on that front. They were the right people to start that fund."

The importance of Halvorsen's early decision to invest cannot be overestimated, according to Odlander:

> "It was a wonderful thing for us to get the backing of not only a large and experienced investor, but in fact the kingdom of Sweden, which provided outstanding validation. The Fourth AP fund is a state body, under scrutiny from government as well as the financial markets, and their support gave many other investors the confidence to join."

Today, 25 years on, HealthCap has about 25 employees, around half of them partners. Although the number of employees has grown, the same mix of complimentary skill sets still exists in the team – experience and knowledge of science, medicine, the capital markets and business are strongly represented among partners and associates.

HealthCap's strength is the same as that of the original founders a quarter of a century ago. Using its range of competencies to find innovations and understand the competitive landscape allows HealthCap to support the development of scientific discoveries that can add huge value to patients, their families and broader society. Additionally, as well as being a thriving business itself, HealthCap has contributed to the creation of many thousands of jobs over the years in its portfolio companies.

After a long and successful career spanning 23 years at the Fourth AP fund, 13 of them as Managing Director, Halvorsen is now retired. During his time at the fund he made many investment decisions, but the decision to back HealthCap sticks out in his mind as special.

"The deal with HealthCap was one of a kind. To be honest, I mostly trusted my gut instinct – and I am happy to say that my feeling was proved to be right."

With an accumulated value of HealthCap portfolio companies to date at around EUR 56 billion, it would seem that Halvorsen's belief in the potential impact of HealthCap was well founded.

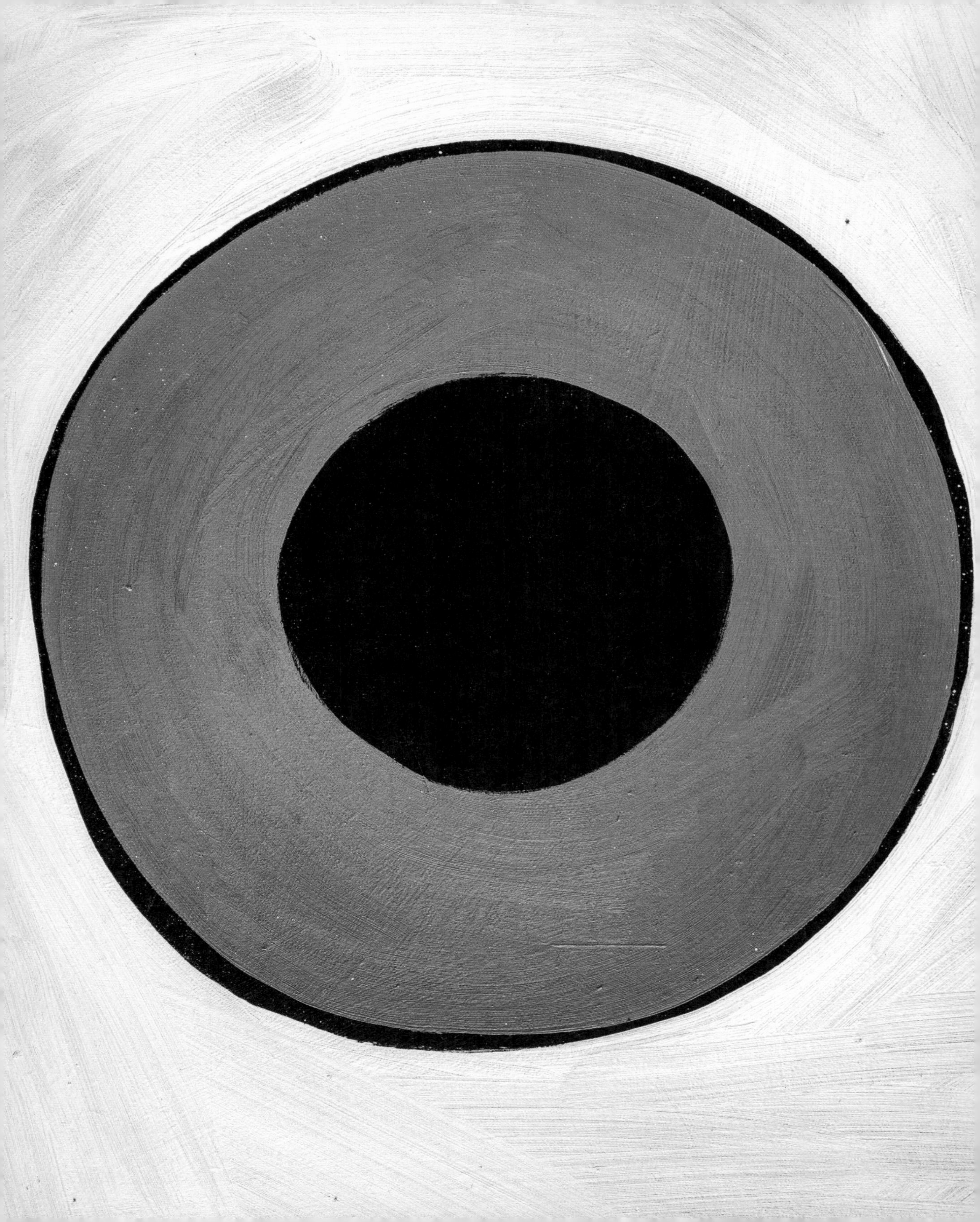

A "Home Run" for Investors

"THAT ASSET WOULD likely never have been developed if it wasn't for HealthCap."

Wilson Therapeutics is one of HealthCap's so-called "home runs" – the trade term for when one company gives a return on investment that pays back the entire fund's capital to investors. Jonas Hansson was CEO of Wilson Therapeutics when it acquired and developed a drug into late-stage clinical development for patients with Wilson Disease. The drug is still on track in development, with the potential to one day become a treatment option that could answer an unmet medical need for patients suffering from this disease, which causes an excessive accumulation of copper in the liver, brain and other organs.

Wilson Therapeutics was set up in 2012 after HealthCap found an asset that had been languishing in the discovery stages of development. Hansson explains:

> "We could see that this was one of those assets that had been 'mistreated', as it had been around quite a long time without getting anywhere. But we saw the potential value if developed properly for the right disease and with the right funding."

The asset, WTX101, first came to HealthCap's attention during the team's normal proactive scouting activities. It represented a potentially novel way of treating Wilson Disease. After months of research, discussion and due diligence, HealthCap purchased the asset and founded Wilson Therapeutics, and appointed Hansson as CEO.

The entrepreneurship of the team at HealthCap was essential to the development of Wilson Therapeutics. Hansson engaged the medical community early on, forming relationships with key opinion leaders internationally. At a centennial celebration meeting held in London, marking the publication of the first monogram about

Wilson Disease, Hansson invited some of the expert speakers to lunch for a brain storming session about developing treatments for the disease.

Michael Schilsky, Medical Director of Adult Liver Transplant at Yale New Haven Transplantation Center, is a specialist in Wilson Disease and attended the lunch:

> "It wasn't a new disease area; Dr John Walshe put the focus on the disease with a revolutionary treatment over half a century ago. But with HealthCap backing, Wilson Therapeutics was really focused on making a difference for patients with this disease."

The collaborative mindset that is part of HealthCap's DNA resulted in a focused strategy and a development programme to build a robust data set that could show the potential of the product to help patients with Wilson Disease.

"When we purchased the asset, we of course believed we had something very interesting," Hansson says, and continues:

> "But it took some time to frame the core value of the asset. We basically had seven large brown boxes of documentation and multiple USB sticks containing data and other documentation, which we sifted through and ordered, so that we could find the right strategic path to effectively move forward with development."

Drug development is complex, and a badly designed development programme can prove costly and effectively stall a product. Like any venture capitalist, HealthCap's aim is to create value in an asset to attract more investment at a higher valuation. After initial private fund-raising rounds, one way of gaining new investors is to grow a company to a value that will attract the public equity markets – and thus pursue a listing through an initial public offering (IPO) on a stock exchange.

After a so-called Series B financing in 2014, which brought in other venture capital investors, Wilson Therapeutics listed on the Nasdaq Stockholm stock exchange in May 2016, attracting healthcare specialist public equity investors. In the same year as the IPO, at a medical conference in Barcelona, Wilson Therapeutics presented preliminary data from the Phase 2 trial that showed improvements in copper control for newly diagnosed adult patients with Wilson Disease who were treated with WTX101.

The drug had already been awarded the status of orphan drug product by the Food & Drug Administration (FDA) in the US, so the new clinical data set created excitement in the Wilson Disease community. Preparations began for a Phase 3 trial and in 2017 the FDA gave the product Accelerated Approval, a status that can expedite the regulatory pathway towards commercialisation. The data also piqued interest in the asset from the pharmaceutical industry and in 2018, soon after the initiation of the Phase 3 clinical trial, the rare disease specialty pharmaceutical company Alexion offered to buy Wilson Therapeutics in an all-cash deal worth USD 855 million (around SEK 7.1 billion). The price represented a 70% premium on the stock price on the day of the offer.

Alexion subsequently expanded the Phase 3 trial with WTX101 (now known as ALXN 1840, and part of AstraZeneca's pipeline after the pharmaceutical giant completed the acquisition of Alexion in 2021) and the study met the primary endpoint of demonstrating improvement of copper mobilisation from tissues.

Schilsky admits he was caught by surprise by the trade sale, but he recognises the deal could provide the product with more resources and stronger international backing in the long run, as well as ultimately a new treatment option for patients. He was, though, sad to see the end to a good collaboration between industry and academia.

"The experience of working with Wilson Therapeutics and the backers at HealthCap was really something very special. It was a good relationship between a company, a CEO and the medical community," Schilsky summarised.

In addition to the Alexion programme, there are currently two additional development programmes ongoing for Wilson Disease, run by Ultragenyx and Vivet/Pfizer, both looking to assess whether gene therapy can correct the underlying genetic defect.

HealthCap partner Mårten Steen, who was on the board of Wilson Therapeutics and is now on the board of Vivet Therapeutics explains:

"Interestingly, HealthCap has long played, and in the case of Vivet continues to play, a part in these programmes being Series A investors in both Ultragenyx and Vivet. It is this that makes it so rewarding as this is a long-neglected patient population which needed new treatment options."

Steen continues:

> "The decision to invest in Vivet Therapeutics was done on the back of the success of Wilson Therapeutics and recognising the unmet medical need of Wilson Disease patients. We understood the opportunity to build a company dedicated to developing a novel gene therapy correcting the underlying genetic cause of the disease. In 2019 Vivet entered an option-based partnership giving Pfizer the right to acquire Vivet for up to EUR 560 million following the completion of Phase 2 studies."

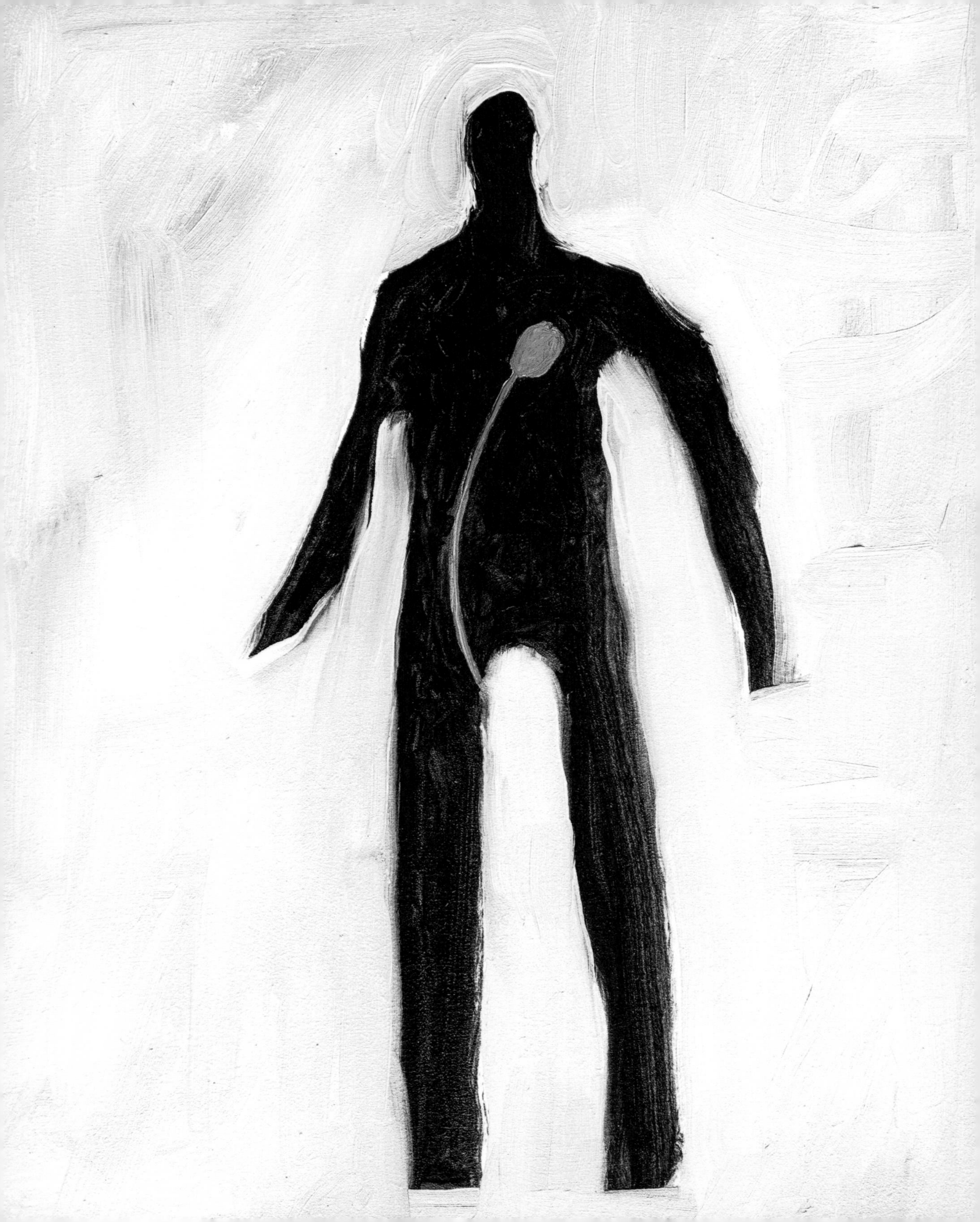

The Importance of Innovation

AS COUNTRIES GET wealthier and populations get older, it is likely there will be increasing demand on healthcare services, and in particular a drive for more focused treatments, as patients and healthcare professionals look to solve unmet medical needs. According to the United Nations' *World Population Prospects* from 2019, it is predicted that globally by 2050 the number of people over the age of 80 will triple and the number of people over 60 will rise to around 2.1 billion.

Scientific understanding and technological capabilities are improving and driving new, innovative solutions within healthcare. The life science industry is witnessing unprecedented levels of innovation in treatment options, processes and regimens – but they come at a cost, something that traditional publicly funded health services cannot bear. Complex research and development programmes to test the safety and effectiveness of novel medical products and devices are expensive. It is here that venture capital funding plays a vital role: in 2020 alone, according to figures published by BioCentury online intelligence, global biotech venture funding was over USD 30 billion, with the majority of investments in the US.

Biochemist Bengt Samuelsson won the Nobel Prize in Physiology or Medicine in 1982. He is convinced of the need for large-scale funding to ensure academic research can reach patients:

> "The most important thing is that we can use new discoveries for new development, which in turn results in new drugs. I am very proud of the discoveries made in academic research, and I see it as an essential part of the ecosystem to have funding from different sources – if you don't have any funding, you cannot do anything."

Venture capitalists such as HealthCap provide this vital start-up funding, as well as development expertise, to turn scientific discoveries into treatments – often ensuring a more personalised approach to address unmet medical needs.

One such area ripe for innovation was cardiology. For years physicians have grappled with the conundrum that although there were treatments for some cardiac issues, older patients could not cope with the invasive procedure of open-heart surgery (which involves opening the chest and cutting through breast bones) in order to have devices inserted that could help their heart condition. It is precisely this kind of unmet medical need that HealthCap is interested in – how to ensure patients can get the help they need in a way that is best suited to them.

After 20 years of performing thousands of open-heart surgeries and authoring more than 200 academic peer-reviewed articles, Professor Jacques Séguin MD PhD founded French-based CoreValve in 2001 to develop a procedure and a product designed to revolutionise the way heart surgery could be carried out.

HealthCap recognised the potential value of the invention and the group's early financial and strategic support resulted in the CoreValve system, using a Transcatheter Aortic Valve Replacement device (TAVR). In simplified terms, a replacement heart valve made from pigs' heart leaflets is attached to a metal net (stent), which is compressed to fit a micro-catheter. This catheter is introduced into the femoral artery and moved into the right position in the heart, where the metal cage is released and unfolds, leading to immediate replacement of the diseased valve with a new functioning one. Hence, a lower-risk procedure enabling older, higher-risk patients to get replacement aortic valves. The system was approved by the European Medicines Agency (EMA) for use in Europe in 2007 and in 2014 in the US, and CoreValve was acquired by Medtronic in 2009 for USD 700 million (around SEK 6 billion).

In recent decades, the importance of venture capital financing in pharmaceutical and medical device development has increased. As an indicator, today, across all HealthCap's portfolio companies there is a combined R&D budget of EUR 400 million. For example, today over 70% of new approved drugs come from the emerging biopharma industry. To keep pharma pipelines full, support for innovation is necessary – but development is expensive, and drug development has a significant failure rate.

Thousands of drug candidates are identified and evaluated for potential use as treatments, with only a fraction of these making it to testing in laboratories or on animals. An even smaller number of potential products are then tested in clinical trials in humans. Estimates for the full cost of developing new drugs from discovery all the way to market are also hard to pin down, but studies in the last five or six years have shown costs to often be in the hundreds of millions of dollars.

Early-stage venture capital funding from the likes of HealthCap ensures the eco-system can flourish, by injecting capital into high-risk scientific innovations which show promise to solve an unmet medical need.

On average HealthCap has helped support 40 clinical trials per year during the last ten years. However, HealthCap also sees a wider impact on society from the ripple effect of investment in early-stage life science innovation. Partner Staffan Lindstrand explains:

> "By supporting early innovative ideas and building companies to develop break-through therapies we not only support efforts to further scientific understanding – thereby improving treatment options for patients and physicians – we also help in the creation of jobs, to provide revenues to governments in the form of taxation and a general increase in experience and understanding of the health-care landscape in society."

Staffan, who has been with HealthCap since 1997, concludes: "And of course, we create returns for our investors, who in turn can reinvest in the sector so that we can pursue even more innovation."

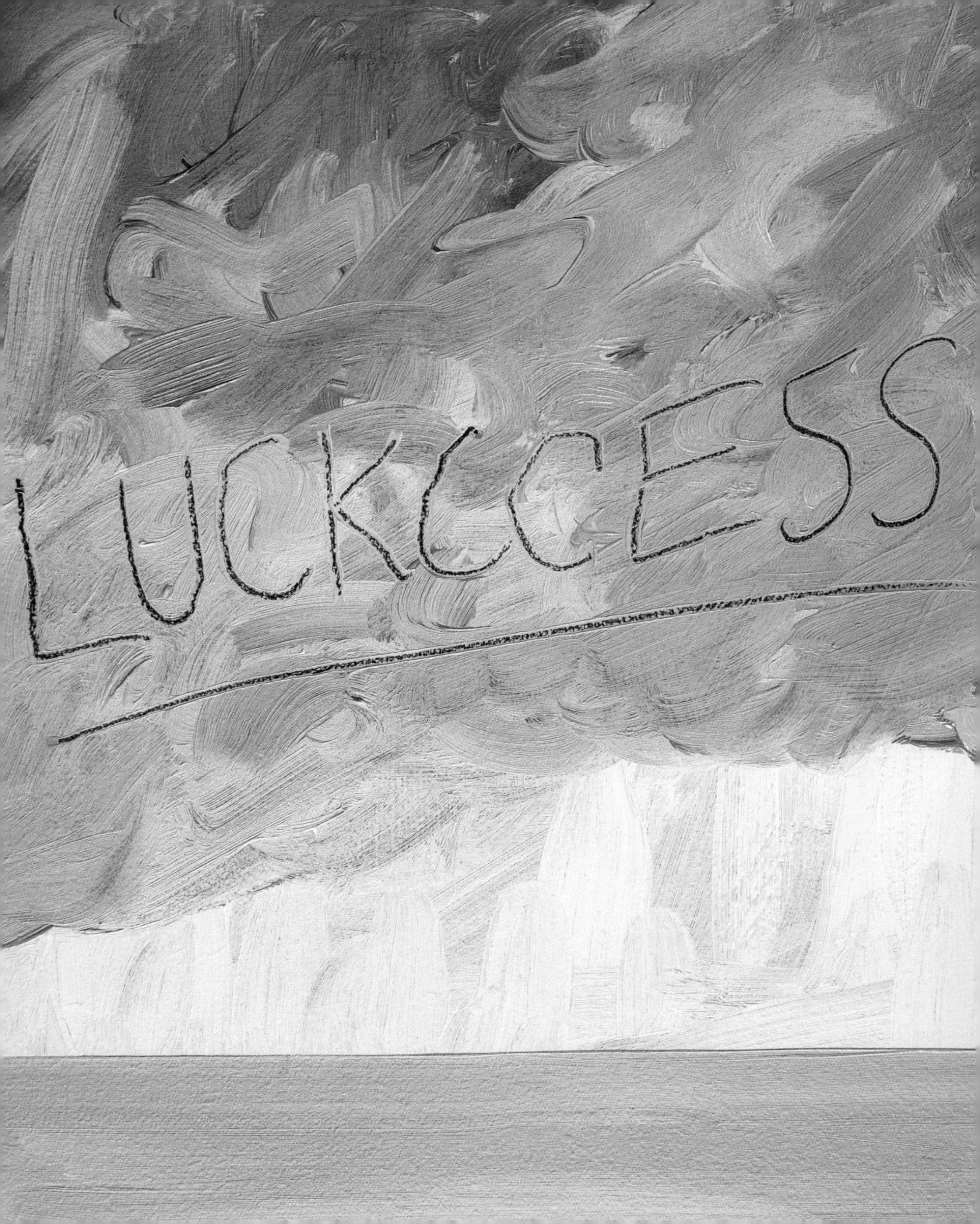
LUCKCESS

Management, Knowledge – or Luck?

BY HIS OWN admission, HealthCap chairman, the industrialist and experienced business executive Per Olof Eriksson, didn't know much about building life science companies, but he recognised the talent and knowledge held by HealthCap's founders and he also understood the idea of spreading risk by investing in a portfolio of companies so that you increase your chances of success:

> "Biotech is such a difficult business from an investor point of view. The strength of HealthCap is that you increase your chances of getting lucky by having very good management and knowledge that can pick a number of companies and invest in them across a fund."

But what exactly is "luck?" Eriksson refers to the great Swedish slalom skier Ingemar Stenmark:

> "It's like when a reporter said that Stenmark was 'lucky to win' and the skier calmly responded, 'I know nothing about luck, only that the more I practice, the luckier I get!' The team and the knowledge base at HealthCap increase the chances of success."

Eriksson has been chairman of HealthCap for the entire 25 years it has been in operation. In 1994, he had stepped out of a job leading the blue-chip engineering and mining group Sandvik, and at the age of 56 was looking for new ways of using his skills in shaping companies, guiding management and building sustainable companies.

When approached by HealthCap's founders Björn Odlander and Peder Fredrikson, Eriksson realised the importance of bringing his skill set from outside of the life science industry to complement the competences of the two founders:

"When I accepted the job as chairman, I did so because I liked the combination and skill sets of Peder and Björn. Biotech wasn't my skill set, and I had no idea how it would fly in the biotech sector, but I was optimistic that this fund was needed as part of the landscape and that these were two people who could make it work."

Despite being a very skilled CEO, Eriksson was humble in terms of how he could best contribute to this new field: "I did, however, make a deal – I wouldn't be involved in the decision-making on which companies to invest in, and I am very happy to have stuck to that decision throughout!"

At the start of the 25-year journey, Eriksson contributed important knowledge on the everyday matter of running a business, as well as lending reputational comfort to investors who had never heard of the fund's two energetic founders, Odlander and Fredrikson.

"I realised I could be of some assistance when they were starting out," he says. "They were not well known, and I had an extensive network. I could help them run a company in a responsible way and, of course, help them raise the funding as they were just starting out."

From those early days in 1996, Eriksson's own role has evolved throughout the quarter-century:

"I really act as a sounding board to the team from everything on structures involved in building a business to succession planning. With a ten–twelve-year horizon for each fund, it is important we have new blood coming into the organisation, but also important that HealthCap's culture is preserved."

Eriksson is proud of the fact that HealthCap has built a team with a formidable set of skills and qualities in-house, so that it can be a respected and effective active investor helping to build the portfolio companies that deliver innovation and create returns for investors. He emphasises:

"The team has a very good reputation – that helps, raising funds and attracting start-ups. The in-house skill set available means they can fully support start-ups in selecting the best opportunities and providing long-term strategic thinking by sitting on boards and management teams where needed."

He continues: "And of course, when it is time for HealthCap to step out from their investment and involvement, the team is hugely skilled in identifying the best *home* for a portfolio company."

Jerini was a company that found a good home when it was acquired by Shire in 2008. Founded in Germany in 1994 and focused on the discovery and development of novel peptide drugs to treat unmet medical needs from its technology platform Peptides-to-Drugs (P2D), the company was helped to grow as a result of HealthCap's early financing and support. The sale to Shire – for EUR 328 million – ensured an important treatment reached patients. Odlander explains:

> "Shire continued to develop Jerini's lead product Firazyr, and the drug is now being used in the US and in Europe treating patients with the terrible, rare disease hereditary angioedema (HAE). This disease is really debilitating as patients experience recurring swelling attacks – for example, in the stomach, face, feet, hands. These attacks can sometimes be life-threatening because of swelling in the throat too. I am very proud that we found such a good home for Jerini and that Firazyr is helping patients."

The sale of Jerini is just one example out of many from which the team has been able to learn during the last 25 years. It is this vast bank of experiences which, according to Eriksson, helps inform decisions taken while investing the VC's funds, the most recent of which is HealthCap VIII: "The funds perform differently. Some perform well, and some, really, really well. Of course, one or two funds have been more challenging."

What has impressed him is that HealthCap has such a broad range of experience to support portfolio companies it invests in:

> "The team offers not only an understanding of the landscape and the science, but also management skills. As well as sitting on boards, some portfolio companies benefit from a HealthCap partner taking the CEO job and developing the organisation in line with the strategy."

For Eriksson, the last quarter-century has flown by. Over the last 25 years HealthCap has backed and built more than 125 companies, raised over EUR 1.2 billion in funds, created 12 unicorns, and taken more than 45 companies public. On top of that there have been numerous industry sales and acquisitions. This, of course, provides a solid foundation for an organisation that is learning and evolving.

The impact has been large, in both the life science sector and in broader society, but Eriksson also savours the memories from the early pioneering days:

"On the night when we were ready to close our first fund, Björn, Peder and I had dinner together, and we were interrupted by a phone call from a member of the well-known Wallenberg family, who announced that they had decided to invest a substantial sum in our fund. It confirmed our feeling: *Now we've started!*"

The Wallenberg family is a Swedish dynasty of industrialists, financiers, politicians and diplomats going back five generations. Today, the so-called "Wallenberg sphere" (from the Swedish Wallenbergsfären) controls, or is a majority owner in, many large international industrial groups with Swedish roots.

In addition to the general economic strength and reputation of the Wallenbergs, the dynasty is a keen supporter of science and research, mainly through the Knut and Alice Wallenberg Foundation, which is one of the largest private research foundations in Europe. To have support from the Wallenberg family was important for HealthCap, both financially and reputationally, and well in line with the family's motto, "To move from the old to what is about to come is the only tradition worth keeping".

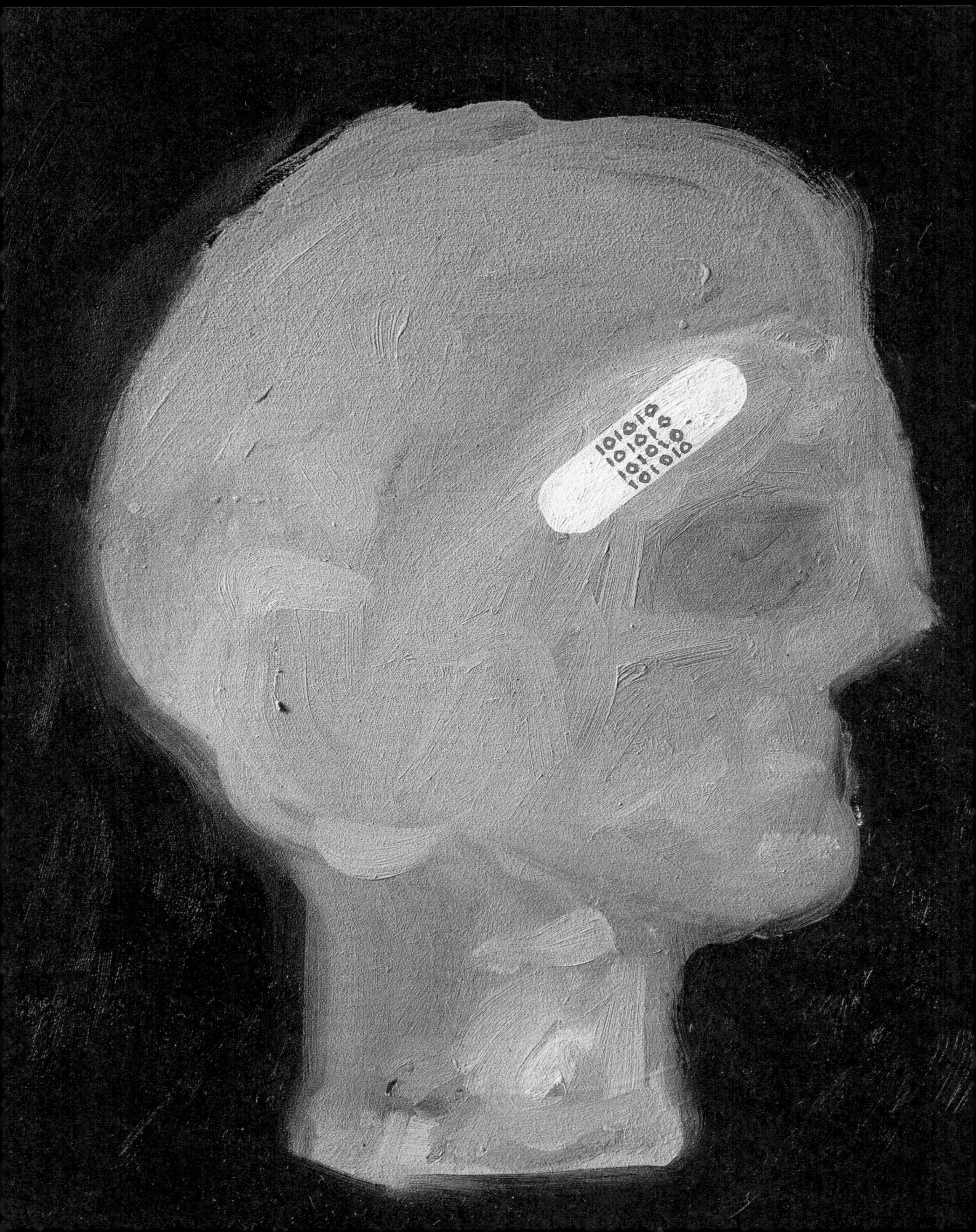
101010
101010
101010
101010

Ready for New Technologies

"RESEARCH IS TO see what everybody has seen and to think what nobody has thought." The quote comes from Albert Szent-Györgyi, a Hungarian scientist credited with the discovery of vitamin C, who in 1937 was awarded the Nobel Prize in Physiology or Medicine.

He was describing the pathway of innovation in the life science sector, where novel discoveries are founded on new understandings in scientific research.

From the discoveries of penicillin, insulin and antibodies in treating cancer, evolution in treatments in the healthcare sector are built on new scientific understanding. By its very nature our approach to healthcare develops with new ideas and innovations, and as a sector it is open to disruption in the form of novel treatment methods or device options. For HealthCap this creates opportunities, with the team asking: "What are the current options and how can we do this more efficiently? How can we use that knowledge to develop better treatments? How can we organise structures more effectively?"

One emerging area keenly followed by HealthCap is innovation that leverages technology. The team firmly believes the future is digital, with new technology offering new opportunities to help impact the life science value chain and lead to better and novel treatment options for patients.

There are many ways for digitalisation to impact healthcare, and not all ideas will end in improvements in treatments, processes or care. However, two of HealthCap's portfolio companies – Doctrin and Orexo – have developed technological innovations that they believe provide benefits for patients, healthcare systems and healthcare employees.

Founded in 2016 in Sweden, Doctrin is digitising the patient experience and journey through the healthcare system from symptom to treatment. Doctrin's digital product is aimed at solving many of the traditional bottlenecks that occur during a patient's interaction with the healthcare system and healthcare professionals.

The HealthCap team does not believe that digitalisation alone will solve problems. They believe that the most value is created when existing care providers still supply care but use digital platforms to increase efficiency and improve the patient experience. Doctrin created a B2B system for healthcare professionals to collect medical histories from patients before the first actual consultation takes place, thereby eliminating the need for multiple face-to-face appointments involving different members of staff.

This focus on both the patient and on healthcare staff was what attracted Doctrin's CEO, Anna-Karin Edstedt Bonamy, who switched from being a practising doctor to join industry: "As a clinician who had also spent time working in how to collect clinical research data, my background seemed very relevant to the vision at Doctrin."

Edstedt Bonamy grew up in a fairly remote part of northern Sweden where her mother was a district nurse. Sweden is, by area, the fifth-largest country in Europe, but it has a population of just 10.4 million people, so she witnessed the challenges in providing healthcare where there is low population density: "I saw first-hand the inefficiencies of having to service patients over a 250-kilometre radius – digital solutions that kept patient care in focus would have changed my mother's working life a great deal."

As a paediatrician, Edstedt Bonamy was frustrated by pure digital players in the market, whose products did not directly enhance the patient experience or provide the right care. Her experiences of working within the healthcare sector gave her an acute sense of how digital tools could be used to improve quality, efficacy and outcome for both the patient and doctor.

Edstedt Bonamy believed that digital tools managed by healthcare professionals for their interactions with patients allow for fact-finding before initial consultations. By collecting medical histories in one place, the tools enable the patient experience to be streamlined when seeing an array of specialists. Perhaps most importantly for the patient, digital tools cut much of the bureaucracy of co-ordinating appointments and turning up to physical meetings at healthcare centres, which can be time consuming and detract from the focus on treatment.

With Doctrin's products, patients document their own medical history, guided at each stage by medical professionals. Edstedt Bonamy explains:

"Doctrin is not *providing* care, that is for healthcare professionals. Our tools *facilitate* care by having a standard process of collecting information in an automated way so healthcare providers can provide care to patients."

This allows more specialists and healthcare professionals to be simultaneously involved in individual patient care. "We can reduce the repetition that patients often experience in the system, where they end up having to tell the same story to different professionals and make multiple visits to different doctors."

Healthcare resources interact across the platform, so the patient experiences a more direct and effective interaction with professionals. "With our tools it is not the healthcare system in the centre, but the patient."

Edstedt Bonamy also points to the contribution that digital data collection can make to a better understanding of different diseases, ultimately helping to improve treatment options for patients.

As a HealthCap portfolio company, the team's support beyond funding has also been vital for Edstedt Bonamy and development at Doctrin.

"HealthCap works a lot with pharma and evidence is important to them. So, although this is harder in digital solutions compared to traditional biotech products, they helped us by providing important expertise on how to put together a model that was customer focused to describe the value created, so we had the right key performance indicators to prove we can provide better solutions."

At the other end of the spectrum, but with the same drivers in force, is Orexo, also working to enhance patient care with digital solutions. Rather than finding a solution to a biological problem via a new drug or delivery method, Orexo developed digital therapies as a resource that could solve the problem of access to treatments for patients with addictions. Nikolaj Sørensen is Orexo's CEO:

"We looked at the disease base – for patients of addictions – and how we could improve the care of the patients. When patients were able to use both behavioural therapy and pharmaceutical treatments, they basically got better results. But we also saw that one of the biggest needs for patients in the US was access to quality counsellors for therapy, and we began to work on how we could solve that need by providing digital therapies for patients."

Orexo now has two marketed digital therapies in the US, Deprexis for treatment of symptoms of depression and Vorvida for the management of problematic alcohol misuse, which complement the pharmaceutical products.

The mix of digital therapies and pharmaceutical products is of growing importance in the healthcare sector, as Sørensen and Orexo have recognised.

> "Regulatory guidelines from both NICE [the UK's National Institute for Health and Care Excellence] and the FDA link psychotherapy and medicine in treatment of addiction, and to have products approved you have to follow a very rigorous programme of testing. For example, Deprexis has been tested in 13 studies comparing the product against other treatments."

Despite some initial resistance from a minority of healthcare professionals and patients, Sørensen believes digital solutions are the way forward in medicine:

> "I would be willing to bet that in just ten years the interaction that you and I have with healthcare will be via a digital interface in many cases. It is a solution to the issue that we have in healthcare of lack of resources."

Doing Well by Doing Good

THE MANTRA OF "doing well by doing good" is at the heart of HealthCap's DNA. The team is committed to contributing to broader society by focusing on breakthrough therapies which provide value to many different stakeholders. To truly live up to the mantra, stakeholders outside of the financial community – in the environment, broader society and governance systems (so-called ESG stakeholders) – also need to be considered. HealthCap partner Anki Forsberg explains that ESG is high on the company's agenda:

> "Several relevant stakeholders, besides fund investors, are important for HealthCap's purpose. Acknowledging and catering to the interests and needs of these stakeholders is important, and we are committed to creating value for a broad spectrum of groups including patients, healthcare systems and society." Forsberg continues: "In line with our core principles, we do this with the utmost compliance with the very strict ethical and regulatory guidelines covering the life science industry."

The belief that success should be rooted in creating value for a broad range of stakeholders has guided HealthCap since the company's foundation. Björn Odlander gives the background:

> "The idea of 'doing well by doing good' has been paramount to us from the beginning. It was important for us to do more than just create a financially successful company. We see HealthCap as contributing to society – and our employees are part of a wider society. As part of this mission, we also aspired to creating a healthy working environment where people were happy and motivated to come to work and felt supported and understood as individuals beyond their jobs."

Odlander continues:

"We realised that we all spent so much time at the office that it was our responsibility to help in finding some sustainable balance between the team's private and work lives. Early on we established a nursery and a playroom next to the conference room, so that 'our' children could come and spend some time with us even when we were at work. As a father myself, I understood the strong emotional pulls beyond the office, and this seemed like a good way of supporting our endeavours. Of course, now it's more common for companies to offer this kind of thing but I'm rather proud that we were somewhat front runners when we did it."

By creating a supportive environment, HealthCap has established a strongly motivated team. Another strong driver for the team is that HealthCap's work does not just create financial success in terms of returns to investors but also offers new options to patients that can improve their quality of life. Likewise, new therapies or medical products that come from investments made by HealthCap can also facilitate potential savings or improve efficiency within healthcare systems. Economic growth is also a by-product of investment in the life science industry, as scientific ideas and innovations help companies to develop products, create employment opportunities and generate revenue to benefit society. This support for broader society is a key driver for the team at HealthCap. Financial success is, of course, paramount, but contributing to society in general is also essential. In order to do well, HealthCap must be doing good for others.

The way each team member approaches and carries out their job is also viewed as important. The life science industry is governed by strict regulations covering drug development, manufacturing and commercialisation, but even beyond these formal rules each employee at HealthCap, and every member of the extended HealthCap family, adheres to a high level of integrity and ethical behaviour.

"We have a comprehensive ethics policy that all of us agree with and sign as part of our employment contracts," says Forsberg and continues: "Fund management is a business based on trust, and we need to stick to the highest standards to avoid, for instance, conflict of interest."

Further, reporting needs to be of the highest standards to create full transparency for investors in the funds, the limited partners (LPs). Forsberg points to the close relationship with the LPs: "We have been lucky and also worked hard to create strong relationships with many international LPs that have continued to back HealthCap over multiple fund cycles."

As HealthCap enters the next quarter-century of its development, the management of ESG factors continues to influence HealthCap's thinking on how to build long-term value for patients, societies and investors. Before each investment is finalised, there is a long process of due diligence where environmental, public health, safety and social issues are considered.

HealthCap ensures these issues are kept firmly in focus by being active owners of portfolio companies and taking seats on their boards. To create a ripple effect beyond the immediate HealthCap family of employees and portfolio companies, HealthCap partners are encouraged to participate in broad networks within public bodies, research institutions and organisations, and other business forums, in order to understand new trends as well as pass on their own experience and skills to others. By doing so, know-how and things learnt from 25 years as a venture capitalist in the life science industry are fed back into broader discussions within science, business, healthcare and how to ensure the sustainability of innovation in the sector.

As Odlander recalls:

> "Now my children are adults and have their own careers. But growing up with HealthCap in the background, they witnessed first-hand that your responsibilities at work cannot be separated from the rest of your life. Contributing in a wider context is essential and also rewarding in many ways."

Harnessing Technology for New Solutions

OREXO, A COMPANY specialising in the field of addiction treatment, is a good example of how understanding the landscape of treatment challenges has led to innovations for potential solutions. Orexo develops improved pharmaceuticals and digital therapies addressing unmet needs within the growing space of substance use disorders and mental health – areas of healthcare that have come under increasing focus due to the impact on individuals of the COVID-19 pandemic. The products are commercialised by Orexo in the US or via partners worldwide.

The main market today for buprenorphine/naloxone products is the US, where Orexo has commercialised Zubsolv as its lead product for the treatment of adults addicted to opioid use. In 2021 the company recorded total net revenues of SEK 565 million and had over 120 employees. The Orexo stock is available to investors on the Swedish stock exchange (the Nasdaq Stockholm) and can also be traded on the OTCQX market in the US. The head office, where research and development is also performed, is situated in Uppsala, Sweden. HealthCap supported Orexo with early funding and the company listed on the Nasdaq Stockholm stock exchange in 2005.

When Nikolaj Sørensen took over as CEO of Orexo in 2013 his background in the pharma industry and previous experience working in management consulting meant he looked through a different lens when considering how to improve outcomes for patients with addiction or depression. Often life science companies are based on a scientific innovation to solve a biological or chemical issue; however, after considering the research identifying the needs of patients to improve outcomes, Orexo adapted its strategy.

"When I first joined," Sørensen says, "we were solving biological problems with a drug delivery approach, where we improved drug formulations to make them more effective. We still do that, but we also looked at the research concerning what was needed to continually improve the care of patients with addictions."

They soon saw that lack of access to treatment was one of the major issues: "It became clear that pharmaceutical treatments work when the patients use them, but access to psychological treatment can improve [the] results of biological treatments, and this access was very limited."

Before the COVID-19 pandemic took hold, it's estimated that in the US alone there were around 16.6 million heavy alcohol users and over 10 million opioid misusers (according to the *National Survey on Drug use and Health* issued in 2018 by the Substance Abuse and Mental Health Services Administration, or SAMHSA), and in 2017 the World Health Organization (WHO) estimated that globally around 264 million people were diagnosed with depression. The need to provide access to counselling services proved a strong motivator for the team at Orexo in its search to develop digital solutions. The event of the global COVID-19 pandemic also further compounded the usefulness of treatment solutions without the need of face-to-face contact with healthcare professionals.

> "Listening to the physicians and patients suffering from addiction it was clear that one of the biggest challenges for patients with addiction diseases in the US was to gain access to quality counsellors. COVID-19 accentuated this situation dramatically as a large share of counselling is managed in group sessions, with COVID-19 this became much more difficult to manage increasing the need for support tools not requiring face to face interaction. Digital therapies provide an answer to this need."

Digital therapeutics utilise high-quality software programs to prevent, manage or treat patients with a broad spectrum of physical, mental and behavioural conditions. They facilitate access to psychological support in a convenient and easy way for patients, and potentially provide access to treatment for a much-wider patient population.

Orexo's primary focus is on the therapeutic areas of alcohol addiction, depression and opioid addiction. The company's commercial products are a mix of so-called traditional pharmaceuticals, with, among others, Modia for use with opioid disorders and Zubsolv the lead product for the treatment of opioid addiction, and two newly approved digital therapies, Vorvida for alcohol misuse and Deprexis for those being treated for depression.

With both pharmacological and digital therapeutics in the clinical offering, Orexo's investment in digital therapeutics has given the company a new cornerstone for future growth driven by these technological solutions.

The effect of the COVID-19 pandemic on the way we lead our daily lives, with the need for social distancing and greater reliance on technology, such as video conferencing and online services, has further underlined the importance of providing support to traditional ways of treating disorders.

In response to the pandemic and recognising the need for remote access to treatment, in April 2020 the FDA introduced an emergency policy for digital therapeutics. The policy was designed to help expand the availability of digital health therapeutic devices for those with psychiatric disorders, which could facilitate consumer use while reducing physical contact and potential exposure to COVID-19.

Even without this move from the FDA, Sørensen was upbeat about the future of digital therapies. He has long believed they are one of the most exciting, as well as rapidly growing, areas within the life science industry. Although payers (that is, insurers, health authorities, and so on) and healthcare providers are still in the early stages of adopting them, Sørensen believes the future is bright:

> "I am confident that as the data continues to show the benefits of a combined approach, any resistance will begin to change over time. Already today, guidelines from NICE and the FDA link improved outcomes to the provision of psychotherapy and medicine."

Sørensen is realistic about why Orexo was able to be a pioneer in the field of digital therapies. The technology was sophisticated enough to be developed into practical products that would be used by patients. He continues:

> "Timing is everything – ten years ago when I was at Pfizer, working in marketing, the technology just couldn't provide the solutions we can offer today, and the patients may not have had broad access to digital technologies. The uptake of smartphones and the innovation in technological solutions in recent years means patients with addiction disorders and depression are now ready to use our products."

Looking ahead, Sørensen believes there is more to come. As well as all the data and research on future needs and trends gathered by Orexo, the CEO points to his own experiences and those of his staff when trying to understand the way that the healthcare sector can develop efficiently and utilise resources in the best way. Sørensen might not be a fortune teller but he still has a clear vision of the future:

> "I am willing to bet that in just another ten years' time the interactions we all have within the healthcare sector will be via a digital interface. The largest challenge we face in healthcare is resources, and with digitisation we can protect the work of doctors by providing a wealth of information for them to help frame the right treatment options for the right patients much more efficiently than today."

The Long and Winding Road

INVESTMENT IN LIFE science innovation causes a ripple effect beyond the investors and companies immediately involved. Networks are formed and knowledge is shared across different communities, including the financial, business, medical and science sectors.

HealthCap contributes to this effect when investing in ideas which fit with the team's long-term, sustainable view of investment. That means funding innovations to benefit patients and their families, while also creating jobs and providing taxation revenue streams for local and national communities. The resources provided by HealthCap, whether alone or by forming syndicates with other investors, allow start-up companies to grow and test their innovation to a level where enough value has been created to attract further financing.

The team at HealthCap is well aware of the responsibilities of steering companies through growth and creating structures that will make them ready to raise more capital via a public listing on a stock market or by being bought by a larger player in the industry, such as specialty or big pharmaceutical companies.

The longevity and collaborative character of the culture at HealthCap has created a sophisticated network of relationships across the financial and academic sectors globally. This in turn has built confidence and trust in the viability of life science companies when listed on the more scrutinised public markets, where the stakes are often higher.

Adam Kostyal is Senior Vice President of Listing Services, Europe, at Nasdaq. He is used to a busy life, juggling his family of five children with his responsibilities at Nasdaq, where he looks after the 800 companies listed on the Nordic Nasdaq exchanges and the 120 European companies that are traded publicly on the Nasdaq market in the US. Kostyal, born in Milan and having worked previously in international companies, has a truly global viewpoint. He enjoys the diversity of collaborating with people from across the world – and he has worked with HealthCap for many years, and respects their long-term perspective:

> "I have seen the entire landscape develop with HealthCap's involvement – both in terms of policy issues and in the way companies are able to grow. HealthCap has a global view and collaborates with other investors via syndicates and creates a circle of trust around different innovative opportunities."

Kostyal continues: "In terms of policy areas, they are focused on creating visibility and confidence in the areas they see will benefit further advancement in the life science sector."

He explains why he believes HealthCap has been able to succeed on the long, arduous road that winds through the financial landscape from start-up to publicly traded company:

> "HealthCap has a more holistic approach to the impact its investments have on the sector. For them it is not just about short-term gains with rate of return on investment. They engage with authorities, financial institutions, regulators and other players to try and ensure scientific innovation can be turned into solutions for unmet medical needs."

Kostyal admits that he is impressed by the way HealthCap works:

> "It's not about raising easy money, but about raising long-term funding. They are long term and want to engage the global sector to build trust and to contribute to policy discussions."

HealthCap's corporate culture is based on respect, collaboration and keeping an eye on the long-term goal. As Kostyal sees it, they want to protect the whole sector.

> "At Nasdaq we discuss with them how they can play an active role in helping to improve the overall market in terms of creating transparency and trust and visibility for these companies – that's one of the key differentiators for HealthCap compared to many other types of investors," Kostyal says, and explains how he looks at HealthCap: "They are a repetitive investor in the sector in the public markets, and they set high standards and help to maintain those standards. In turn this brings expertise and knowledge and builds confidence in investing in

the sector." But, of course, no one is perfect, Kostyal smiles: "I am sure they have made mistakes and surprised companies or other investors in some cases, but on the whole they stand on very high ground from a reputational perspective."

When HealthCap started in 1996 it was a pioneer in the Nordic market, both in providing sector specific investment for the life science sector and for taking a long-term view.

Within the life science sector, where product development is expensive and high risk, venture capital funding is necessary to develop anything viable. Venture capital is a form of financing that is provided to start-up companies and small businesses that are judged to have long-term growth potential. The financing is regularly combined with active ownership and valuable know-how. The money is pooled in funds and comes from various sources, including high net-worth private investors, pension funds and other financial institutions. To date, HealthCap has raised over EUR 1.2 billion from over a hundred institutional investors.

As Kostyal emphasises:

"Venture capitalists are an essential part of the landscape as they provide vital funding so that start-ups can bring their ideas to a level where more funding can be attracted. For example, via a public listing. What HealthCap has been really good at is being at the interface of exciting science that could provide a solution to an unmet medical need and helping founders develop their businesses, so processes and strategies add value which then attracts further funding for further development."

HealthCap has, he says, also left a deep footprint on the global public markets:

"Having been involved in an astonishing number of IPOs – more than 40 – where a company goes from being private to offering its shares to be traded on a public stock exchange, HealthCap brings great experience to entrepreneurs and to investors in how to manage the life cycle of these companies in a sector that is very volatile. They are not just investors but also feel a responsibility to be a coach, owner and sounding board for building value in the long term."

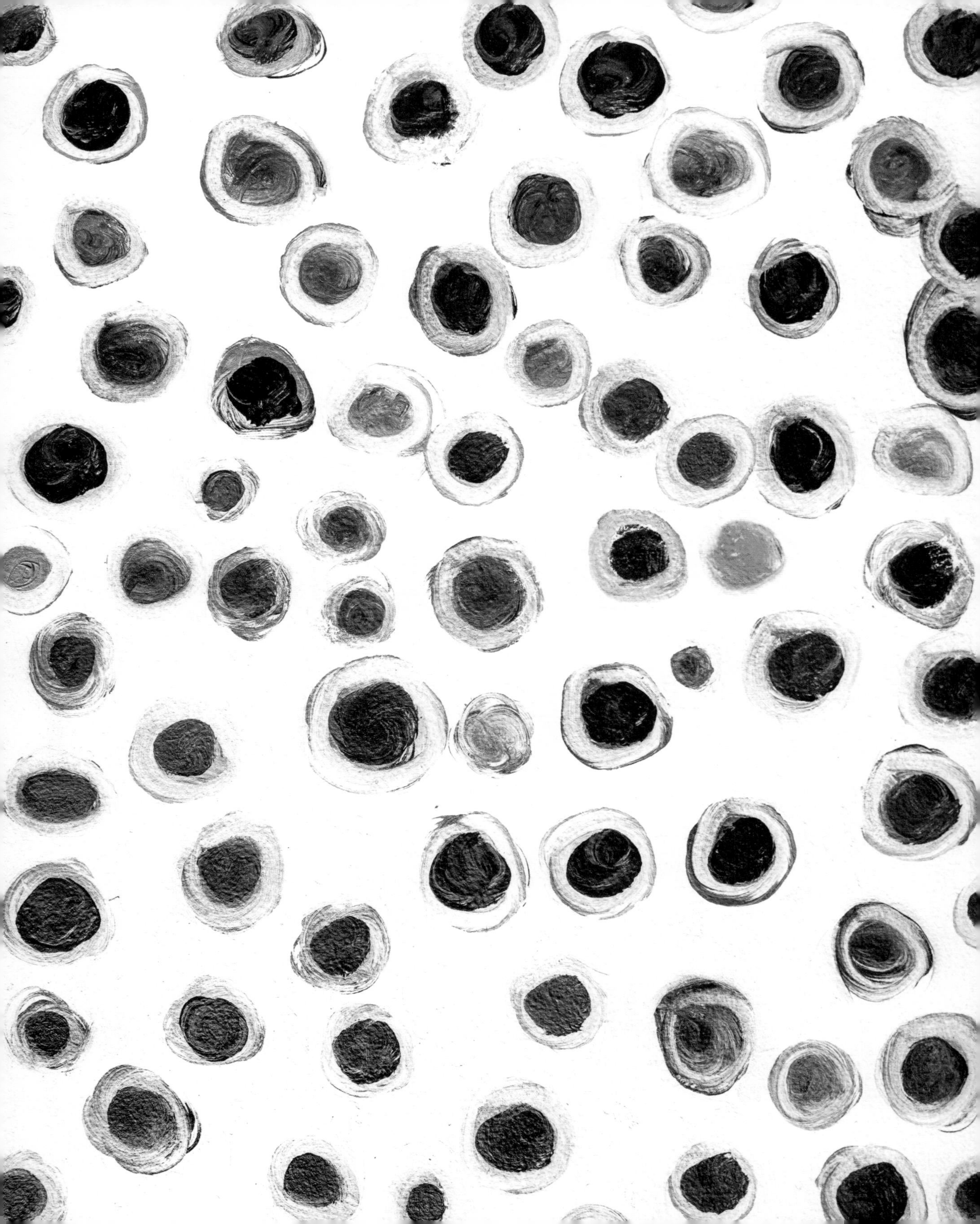

Crucial Funding for Innovation

HEALTHCAP WAS STILL in its infancy when the financial markets – and valuations – came crashing down around them during the crisis in the markets caused by the end of the internet bubble at the turn of the millennium.

In 1996, when Björn Odlander and Peder Fredrikson were starting out, HealthCap was pretty much a lone wolf as a northern European venture capital fund. The bursting of the tech and biotech bubble just a couple of years later could have persuaded them to throw in the towel. However, they were convinced that there was a need for venture funding for life science innovation anchored out of Europe, so they kept going, and learnt from steering their ship through the crisis. Odlander recalls:

> "Back then we really had to take some deep breaths. We were fairly new in the game and didn't have the track record and experience we have today. We look at the global COVID-19 pandemic that swept across the world in the last years and although the situation was extremely serious our experience over the years meant that we were able to steer a way through so we could reach the light at the end of the tunnel."

By taking deep breaths and calming each other, the team was able to keep sharp focus on its core competencies and strategy to survive the tech-bubble burst, as well as subsequent crises including the 9/11 terrorist attacks on the World Trade Center towers in Manhattan in 2001.

Venture funding was more mature in the US and although activity dipped with the millennium market crash, the industry rebounded. US venture capitalism had emerged out of the private equity investor landscape during the 1960s and 1970s, and many of the start-ups that were funded then have grown into the tech giants of Silicon Valley today.

Uli Grabenwarter, Head of Venture at the European Investment Fund (EIF), which is part of the European Bank Group, was all too aware of the need for European venture capital (VC) funding in sectors across the board as well as in life science. He was also conscious of the terrible timing of trying to encourage such funding at the time of a market crash. Back then, Grabenwarter had just joined the EIF in a role aimed at building up venture funding in Europe.

"When I joined, we were full of optimism that we could place the European venture market on the map as a serious asset class and were looking at our investment strategy for the year ahead," he remembers, "but by the time we were done defining our priorities for the year to come the market had disappeared due to the tech-bubble bursting."

But according to Grabenwarter, HealthCap's global outlook and deep knowledge in the sector gave it an edge that allowed it to weather the storm and survive: "HealthCap was one of the few European VCs that made it through the Death Valley of the market situation after the crash in 2000."

Grabenwarter laments the fact that although globally venture funding was washed into the shallows due to the millennium crash, the VC sector in the US bounced back whereas Europe took a decade to recover and still has a significant gap to close compared to the US today.

> "Currently, Europe's VC market is only about a quarter of the VC market in the US, which no doubt is better than back in 2000 when it was only a tenth. But more surprisingly, VC funding in Asia, which was virtually non-existent back in 2000, has caught up with the US in the last two decades, while Europe still hasn't. That evolution needs to make us think."

HealthCap, as the leading VC fund in northern Europe, has helped to raise awareness of the pressing need for and benefits of this type of funding for investors in the European life science sector. According to Grabenwarter, who looks through a broader lens of VC funding across multiple sectors, the reason we have not seen the creation of monolithic companies in the tech sector in Europe, for example (in the same way as in the US), is because of the lack of capital available to be invested in start-ups in Europe.

> "We do have a bunch of unicorns in Europe, but we have not managed to make them grow to a weight in the technology markets where they basically have an influence on what technology makes it and to which markets. They aren't able

to be as dominant as the tech companies such as Amazon, Facebook and the like. To achieve that, European companies require capital far beyond what is currently available."

Although European VC life science funding has increased over the last decade, it still lags behind levels invested by US VCs in the sector. In 2019 VCs in Europe invested around USD 3 billion in life science innovations, while US VCs invested almost four times as much, at USD 12 billion. The rest of the world is also ramping up investment from VC sources. Including VC investment from China and other areas, global VC funding in the sector totalled more than USD 18.8 billion in 2019.

One of the constraints on the levels of European VC funding may be the perceived high risk of failure of innovations within the life science sector, which puts off traditionally rather conservative investment institutions in Europe. Likewise, pension funds and insurance companies often follow fixed income strategies that more conveniently meet their liquidity needs compared to the long-term development horizons and funding needed to support life science innovation.

Yet, Grabenwarter demonstrates with impressive figures from the EIF's portfolio across all VC-backed industries that life science investments outperform any other market segment, even on a risk-adjusted basis. However, investors need to have a particular mindset when investing in life science compared to technology innovations. Grabenwarter believes that investors need to understand the process and long-term horizons needed to bring life science innovation to commercialisation. They also need to manage the binary nature of scientific breakthroughs in life science through appropriate diversification:

"There is a long-term nature to the business models and there are specific challenges for product development in this area. This is different to the tech sector, where business models show value building consistently, but in the life science industry the value is much more binary with each step – it either flies or it dies. This calls for superior selection skills and sound diversification of portfolios."

When considering the healthcare sector in particular, Grabenwarter is convinced it is moving more and more in the direction of specificity of treatments and this should play into the strengths of HealthCap.

"One core focus of HealthCap has always been on orphan drugs," he explains. "For many years such a focus was perceived as not being lucrative within the industry, as the markets for such drugs or devices were too narrow. Now, when we are in an era where blockbuster drugs are gradually replaced by personalised therapeutic treatment strategies, the entire therapeutic research sector is being reshaped."

Healthcare is a global industry, and to succeed in growing companies and bringing innovation towards the market, a deep knowledge of the scientific and business competitive landscape internationally is essential to create the best chances of success for investors – something HealthCap has been acutely aware of. To date around 3 million patients have been treated with therapeutics or medical devices developed by HealthCap portfolio companies. As Grabenwarter stresses:

"Global detailed knowledge on the competitive landscape is key when investing in disruptive innovation in technology. In an investment context, you simply cannot afford, three or four years down the line, that the company you have invested in won't fly because there are more competitive business models out there that are overtaking yours."

Innovation is costly and takes time, and innovation in the life science sector can be particularly lengthy. Not all ideas will turn out to be successes that can benefit society, and the funding needs to support such early innovation are large. Venture capital funding is just one of the options that needs to be available to support innovation.

HealthCap followed a well-defined business model focused on supporting innovation in the life science sector for unmet medical needs in rare diseases. Its global perspective on the competitive landscape and scientific innovations has helped it weather the various ups and downs in the market over the past 25 years, build a sustainable business and take the title of leading VC in northern Europe.

"For the last 15 years VC funding has been a core ingredient for technological innovation. Today, policymakers and governments have understood how pivotal the role of venture capitalist funding is to foster innovation, and they are increasingly relying on such funding to help build sustainable societies in the face of the global challenges we encounter," Grabenwarter concludes.

WELL
WELL
WELL

WORK HARD
AND
BE NICE
TO
PEOPLE

The Sum of the Parts

> "A few years ago, our offices were visited by the king of Sweden, Carl XVI Gustaf. That was amazing in itself. But when I held the door open for the king as he was leaving, Björn introduced me by name to the king. I think that shows what a special culture we have here at HealthCap – I was just holding a door, but for Björn I was part of the team which the king was visiting."

THE KING'S VISIT followed a Royal Technology Mission to the US in May 2017, of which Björn Odlander had been part. The story is told by Gunilla Byström, a longe-serving employee at HealthCap. She joined in 1997 and now runs the office and organises HealthCap events.

It's a sentiment echoed by the 25 or so employees employed at HealthCap today – partners, associates and back-office staff alike. This special culture is what makes them come to work each day. The work is interesting, the company has a meaningful purpose and there is a respectful atmosphere. The strength of the team is the culture that binds them together – everyone contributes to success and is committed to another HealthCap company mantra: "Work hard and be nice to people."

In reputational surveys it's not uncommon for companies such as banks and investment funds to rank low on the scale. The value added by venture capitalists, investment bankers and others working in the financial sector is often questioned by outsiders. In the healthcare sector there can be an even greater scepticism, with the familiar accusation that investors are simply creating profit from the needs of people who are ill or disabled.

Alex Valcu, partner at HealthCap, summed up his own concerns about working in the finance sector before he joined HealthCap, and how the company bucked the trend:

> "Back in the early days, I had no intention to work in the finance sector. My view was that I would never fit in. When I was approached by HealthCap, I decided to give it a shot, and I haven't regretted it. I've learnt that there are exceptions and I'm proud to be part of one of them, where people, well-being and innovation are the key words."

Valcu came to HealthCap in 2004 after working in IT and his story is not unique. HealthCap runs a small, almost a family office, type of organisation – a "boutique" investment firm where the founders have shared their passion for business with all employees, whatever their role in the firm, and have a very close relationship to all their external stakeholders: investors, researchers and employees in portfolio companies. At a time when reporting and compliance within the finance sector have become more and more pervasive, HealthCap complies with all regulatory obligations while continuing to maintain strong personal relationships.

Another member of the team who values the culture at HealthCap is Head of Compliance Marile Schiess. She first met the team when working as an auditor at EY, and when they called asking her to join the company in 2016 she jumped at the chance.

> "It is inspiring to work with people who are passionate and dedicated to their work and life and that add significant value to many stakeholders - patients, physicians, society, portfolio companies, owners, employees as well as investors."

This sentiment is echoed by colleague and senior controller at HealthCap, Mikael Grundström, who has been at the company for 16 years:

> "Healthcap's beliefs, values and sense of purpose lifts the company above many others. I look forward to continuing the journey together with my colleagues."

HealthCap's current head office at Engelbrektsplan in Stockholm has a view over that famous park bench in Humlegården where, in 1996, Odlander and Fredrikson started HealthCap. In 1998 the company expanded with an office in Lausanne in Switzerland. According to Fabrice Bernhard, a general partner based in the Swiss office, it is this focus on individuals and people that makes the difference:

> "When collaborating with HealthCap, you develop an inter-personal relationship with real, dedicated people. As an investor, you are not only getting dry reporting from a service centre, you have a real-life person as a partner liaising with investors and providing tailored information, and there are always direct lines open when in need for a private contact to be established. For our portfolio companies, it is not just money coming from an impersonal fund, but a partner, a flesh-and-blood advisor, who is deeply involved in the development of business by sharing previous experience in the field."

Bernhard explains that the downside of these close relationships is that it can be hard to say goodbye to portfolio companies when the time comes for HealthCap to realise its investment.

> "As a venture capitalist we have to make our investment grow and we have to exit. But when that time comes it is certainly never an easy task for those involved to let their baby go, but this is what we do and the strong relationships made over the years remain and often provide new opportunities due to the deep and trusted network that was built over the years."

Byström's story about the royal visit also shows how HealthCap has chosen employees to join the team based on their skills, personality and experience. Byström joined the firm when she wanted to take time out from her work on cruise ships. She was looking for a change and Odlander saw the skill set and intelligence that Byström could bring to manage the HealthCap office effectively. In her previous roles Byström had shown she could deal with international clients in a respectful and friendly way, she was professional, helpful and solution focused.

Byström was highly motivated by the company's culture of respect and hard work, as well as the purpose of doing good for others, and decided to join the team. At the time she was used to six-month contracts on cruise ships, but Odlander persuaded her to sign on for longer. She's never looked back.

"We are not a huge team," she says, "but we have made a huge impact on improving patients' lives. I am proud because we are not first and foremost digging for gold, we are digging for healthy strong companies that want to help patients to be able to live better lives."

Sitting in the conference room in the Stockholm office she recaps:

"During my many years at HealthCap I have made hundreds of bookings for partners and the whole company, and I have often received the feedback that we are 'a nice bunch'! I am proud to work among kind, nice professional people, where we are also creating something good for other people."

Likewise, Sofie Wennerqvist was an early member of the team, joining in 2002 as a receptionist when taking a break from life as a pre-school teacher. Now Wennerqvist is responsible for taking care of much of the back-office administration, ensuring compliance and the tracking of the portfolio holdings, and that the shares and options agreements are in place. When she was first interviewed by Odlander, Byström and Anki Forsberg, one of the original partners, Wennerqvist was looking for breathing space from life in the classroom. The focus on people in the team is a strong motivator for her:

"At HealthCap they invest in people. It's a small company so it is so important to find the right type of person to be hired. The people here take their time to teach and develop people – not just in the organisation itself but also in the portfolio companies. The relationships I now have with our portfolio companies and others are part of our strong culture of creating networks and learning from the experience of others."

The relatively small team helps to keep everyone at HealthCap in touch with the impact the VC has on the life science sector. With everyone doing their bit, the sum of the parts makes a strong and valuable whole.

"We can work independently and have individual responsibility, but we all contribute to the team and the atmosphere is good. The culture is so strong, a mixture of kindness and professionalism, and that's probably why I am still here after so many years."

As venture partner Georg Beiske states: "We play a role in bringing medical innovation forward. We support strong science and are willing to risk the resources required to give good ideas a real chance at becoming a product that can help patients."

HealthCap has also created a ripple effect in the Nordic region, forming relationships with other VCs across the region as well as internationally, and encouraging a widespread boost to innovation in the life science sector. As Valcu puts it:

"We have played a vital role in the Nordic life science industry for 25 years, supporting innovation and attracting other professional capital to the region. Nordic life science would not be the same today without HealthCap."

HealthCap's strong culture means it can hand-pick new talent to add to the core of employees to strengthen the team's skill set and ensure the sustainability of the business. Expansion of the team is done cautiously though, and over time. Partner Per Samuelsson states:

"Our culture is built carefully. We are conscious of the need to do succession planning. We expand the team slowly, making sure any addition has the right skill set and personality to be part of the HealthCap team – we also have to like them on a personal level."

Along these lines of careful organisational development, Dr Mårten Steen in 2021 was promoted to co-managing partner. Mårten joined HealthCap in 2005 as a medical associate and departed for a tenure in business development at the pharmaceutical company Merck Serono. He returned to become partner in 2010 and has been instrumental in many of HealthCap's most successful investments.

"It is wonderful to be part of creating and supporting the next generation of companies developing breakthrough therapies," says Steen. "Our endeavour has the potential to be transformative for patients around the world."

The average tenure of HealthCap employees today is around 16 years, which is unusual in a sector where rapid job switches are commonplace. As HealthCap partner Eugen Steiner says, once you become part of the team there is little incentive to work elsewhere.

"What makes this organisation great is the opportunity to work with all these amazing people – the partner group and all our co-workers, the brilliant scientist-inventors and the many people who contribute to the development of new healthcare products," Steiner says, and continues with a smile: "I realise this sounds a bit clichéd, but nevertheless – that's what's kept me here for almost 25 years!"

Taking the Fight to Cancer

CANCER IS ACTUALLY at least 200 different diseases, effectively making the condition a basket of "rare diseases", and with around one in five men, and one in six women globally predicted to develop cancer during their lifetime, it is likely we will all know someone affected by cancer at some point during our lives.

Cancers are diseases where uncontrolled cell growth damages the body's normal tissues. Cancer can affect many different parts of the body, including skin, bone, fat, muscle, the immune system and blood. Intensive cancer research in recent decades has led to many different treatments being approved in recent years, so that in many cases patients can live with their cancer rather than losing their lives to the disease. However, with 9.9 million deaths worldwide in 2020, there are still many unmet medical needs in cancer.

With its dedicated focus on finding solutions to unmet medical needs, HealthCap has been at the forefront of supporting oncology companies during discovery and early research. Drug development is never a straight line, and when they hit bumps in the road, venture capitalists and scientists need to keep focused on the goal – finding a way forward for a therapy that will help patients.

A good example of this within HealthCap's portfolio is Oncopeptides, an international oncology company headquartered in Sweden. Oncopeptides focuses on the development of targeted therapies for difficult-to-treat haematological diseases. The company was started in 2000, based on research from leading Swedish cancer scientists and got its first commercialised product in early 2021 when the US FDA approved melflufen for the treatment of relapsed and refractory multiple myeloma patients under the brand name Pepaxto. The drug is a so-called peptide drug-conjugate that works by entering myeloma cells, where the drug conjugate is broken up and rapidly releases an alkylator causing cell damage and eventual cell death.

However, the FDA's interpretation of data from a post-approval confirmatory study with melflufen (the phase 3 OCEAN study) put a spanner in the works and triggered a shareprice plunge and sent the company's leadership back to the drawing board to reassess the future of the product. Pepaxto was voluntarily withdrawn from the US market and Oncopeptides began a deepened analysis of the data from the OCEAN study while reorganising the company back to the R&D focus of earlier years. HealthCap believed melflufen might still have a role in the multiple myeloma treatment landscape, and stood by Oncopeptides' efforts to see if a new pathway for melflufen could be found.

In parallel with the above, Oncopeptides applied for a conditional approval of melflufen in the EU with the EMA, the EU's regulatory authority for medcines – a process that was ongoing at the time of publishing. Additionally, after rigorous data mining in the OCEAN trial andother related clinical trials Oncopeptides revoked its voluntary withdrawal from the US market with the aim of pursuing a dialogue with the FDA regarding the future for Pepaxto in the US.

As Per Samuelsson, partner at HealthCap explains, the role of venture capital is to keep focus on scientific data and the potential of innovation to provide a new treatment option. "Oncopeptides is a good example of how the pursuit of solving unmet medical needs support from investors. Drug development takes time, scientific brainpower and understanding, and it is imperative to provide the capital to support a robust development approach."

Since the early days of Oncopeptides, HealthCap played an important role in the development of the company. Together with a small number of other initial investors, they provided much-needed capital as well as a sounding board, to help Oncopeptides progress this new approach to hard-to-treat cases of multiple myeloma.

The journey the company has been on, including rapid success, disappointment, and a return to the foundation of science to find a new path forward for the drug illustrates what VC often is about.

In the first ten years, the company was research focused and product development was slow. In 2011, Jakob Lindberg, who is currently the CEO at Oncopeptides and was a key driver in the development of the lead product, was looking at the potential for advancing the research into a product that could be used to treat certain rare oncology diseases. Lindberg, who has both a scientific and business background, explains:

"Chemotherapy was basically born out of the US military's attempts to create a chemical weapon. They found a way of killing cells, which academic researchers adopted to become early-stage, so-called alkylator-based chemotherapy to counter cancer. Long story short, skilful researchers in Sweden managed to take one type of alkylator, which had been around since the 1960s – called melphalan, and add an amino acid to create a peptide. And this became the lead product melflufen."

During the early stages of the company the scientists focussed on research and the creation of patent protection for the product candidate. It then became obvious that for the next stage of development it was important to add individuals skilled and experienced in the industrialisation of product development.

"When I joined the company, I understood we would need to focus the development plan and then have new funding to develop the product correctly," Lindberg says, "so I started talking to HealthCap, who I knew would understand the potential of the product."

Up to that point, pre-clinical work at Oncopeptides was backed by the development arm of Sweden's Karolinska Institutet and Industrifonden, another of Sweden's venture capital firms, a fund that originally was set up by the Swedish government in 1979. However, when Industrifonden took complete ownership of the company in 2012 HealthCap saw the opportunity to push the development of melflufen into the clinic and came in as a partner.

With HealthCap's investment came two seats on the Board of Directors, allowing the team to bring strategic focus and development expertise to the table. A small Phase 1 study had been carried out prior to 2012, but as Samuelsson had assessed, more proof was needed to be able to bring the asset forward.

"There had been a clinical study," he recalls, "but it wasn't really designed so that we could continue to build on the results. Instead, we discussed how to best build shareholder value, and in which disease indications to test the drug, and then we started to design a clinical programme that would generate evidence concerning the effect of the drug."

With funding from Industrifonden and HealthCap, as well as from other members of the board and management, Oncopeptides embarked on the initial studies of melflufen in late-stage multiple myeloma patients, to provide a more robust data set. On the back of data from these studies, melflufen was granted orphan drug status in both the US and EU allowing certain advantages including extended exclusive marketing rights.

Multiple myeloma is a disease where recent new drugs have helped patients to live longer with their disease. In Samuelsson's view this makes the need for improved drugs even more apparent:

> "Multiple myeloma is not just one disease, and it is often said it changes during its duration. Doctors treat patients for many years and since patients get refractory [resistant] to the treatments, they need a palette of drugs with different modes of action. They currently don't have a one-stop-shop option, so they look for treatments that can be added to their toolbox in order to continue treating their patients."

Oncopeptides was in a period of strong momentum, and the next step was to raise more funds by taking the company public. It is part of HealthCap's strategy to ensure all portfolio companies plan for an eventual public listing, or IPO (initial public offering). In Oncopeptides' case, the decision to go public was made quickly, in 2016, to take advantage of the market situation and secure funding for the next stage of development. As Samuelsson states:

> "We could never have funded a costly Phase 3 trial on our own, or the next steps needed to get the product on the market, so this was the logical step. But it went quickly – I think it was one of the fastest processes ever for an IPO. From the day we had the kick-off meeting with the banks to the day it was listed on the Stockholm stock exchange was just shy of five months."

Although the science was in place, there were still some corporate structures that needed to be created in order for the company to be publicly listed.

> "It was not quite a public company from a structural point of view. So, in that short time we built and added the features that were needed. Quickly. Infrastructure, key members of the team, everything that you need to make the company fully ready to be publicly listed."

The IPO in February 2017 raised the large sum of SEK 650 million, with a starting stock price of SEK 46 per share. The stock price increased over 70% in the first

12 months of trading, showing there was large support from investors in the public equity markets. As a positive side effect, the Oncopeptides IPO also bolstered the sentiment in the Nordics that the region's rich cancer expertise and innovation culture could be tapped and turned into real value for investors and patients.

When building a company, the Board of Directors needs to be looking to the years ahead. During 2019 as the company was ramping up the strategy to commercialise its first product, Lindberg began thinking about stepping aside from the top job and returning to his passion of leading R&D strategic development. HealthCap reluctantly agreed, and appointed Marty J. Duvall, a seasoned pharma and biotech executive with commercial experience, to be the new CEO. Lindberg explains:

> "The CEO job is lonely, and at that point in our development, on the brink of commercialisation, the next stage of company growth would have meant me spending 50 per cent of my time in the US."

However, when melflufen hit some roadblocks after approval in the US, it became clear that Lindberg's talents in drug development were again much needed to lead the strategy at Oncopeptides – so he took up the CEO reins once more in 2021.

The journey to reposition melflufen is ongoing. Both HealthCap and Jakob Lindberg are confident of the potential of the drug and the role it can play in treating certain types of multiple myeloma.

As Samuelson says:

> "Jakob's drive and motivation, as well as his scientific insights are crucially important at this time for Oncopeptides. This is an important time for the company and we were very pleased that Jakob agreed to again to take the strategic lead to navigate the next steps for melflufen."

A Mastermind of Venture Capital

ONE OF THE most influential venture capitalist investors in the US, Frank Caufield, played a key role in shaping the development of HealthCap from inception to thriving business. Björn Odlander, founding partner of HealthCap, reflected on his relation to Caufield:

> "Frank was a very special person. He was an incredibly talented businessman, but he was also a larger-than-life character committed to enjoying himself while also doing things that mattered in the world. His support and advice was instrumental to the success of HealthCap, and I am very grateful for all he did for the firm and for me personally."

From the early 1970s Caufield was a co-founding partner at what is arguably one of the most successful venture capital firms, Silicon Valley's Kleiner Perkins Caufield & Byers (KPCB), now Kleiner Perkins. Being an investor in more than 900 early companies, KPCB paved the way for what has today become a thriving VC sector on the West Coast of the US.

Odlander, Fredrikson and Caufield first met in the summer of 1995 when Frank Caufield was visiting Stockholm together with Jim Kimsey, the founder of AOL (America Online). Caufield was a member of the AOL Board of Directors and KPCB had been a founding investor in the company.

After being introduced by Lou Gerken, Fredrikson's friend and former partner, Odlander invited them on a cruise in his old motorboat in the archipelago around the Swedish capital.

"It was a beautiful summer day and Stockholm presented herself at her best. It was a very down-to-earth and friendly afternoon on the water – probably very different from the other parts of their trip." Odlander remembers the day fondly: "We ended the day with smorgasbord at Ulriksdal's Inn, a waterfront restaurant north of Stockholm, and then a nightcap downtown."

It was to be the start of a mentorship and friendship between the two that lasted until Caufield's passing in November 2019.

When Odlander and Fredrikson launched HealthCap in 1996, Caufield became a trusted advisor, and he remained an active supporter and sounding board for the firm for many years. His impact on HealthCap was not limited to business advice; his personality also echoed the atmosphere and tone of the Swedish VC's corporate culture, says Odlander:

> "We were just a start-up in the venture capital world, and Frank's stature in the sector gave us both credibility and kudos. But what was most valuable was his strategic insight and very straightforward way of communicating. He brought focus and clarity – and also humour – even when times were challenging."

Caufield's good-natured personality combined common sense with a sharp analytical and strategic mindset. At the time of his death, Brook Byers, fellow co-founder at KPCB, said:

> "Frank had so many talents, he had both wisdom and wit, so that a lunch or a dinner with him was both a master class in business strategy as well as an illustration of how you can use humour to bring honesty and simplicity to discussions."

KPCB was formed in 1972 when Caufield and Byers joined forces with Eugene Kleiner and Tom Perkins to form a united venture capital firm focused on funding innovations in technology and life science. KPCB invested in some of Silicon Valley's best-known success stories, including Genentech, AOL, Compaq, Netscape, Amazon and Google.

Caufield's route into venture capitalism was not typical. As a child he lived in different parts of the US, and in Spain as well as in the UK, as his father pursued military postings. His experiences during these formative years were influential in shaping his character, as well as his understanding and curiosity of different cultures. He followed his father into the military and studied at the United States Military Academy at West Point, graduating in 1962.

Odlander believes that Caufield's broad experiences during his formative years enabled him to look at things from different angles and bring in valuable perspectives:

> "Frank's background was so varied, and this gave him unique insights when looking at how to build a business. As well as his obvious experiences and skills as an investor and partner to growing businesses, he was also a military man, with an incredibly broad network in government and the armed forces as well as the investment landscape."

He was also a master of one-liners, and Odlander clearly remembers the pithy advice given by Caufield in the face of the approaching financial crisis: "Hunker down, apply Ho Chi Minh tactics, stay alive."

After several postings, including working in military intelligence in Germany, he felt the call of the business world and in 1966 he resigned his commission to attend Harvard Business School. Despite leaving the military, the friendships he forged during his time at West Point and in service would remain important throughout his life.

As well as achieving success in the venture capital sector, he served as president of the Western Association of Venture Capitalists and the National Venture Capital Association, and was also an active community philanthropist, supporting and serving on the boards of the Council for Foreign Relations, Child Abuse Prevention Society of San Francisco, the US Russia Investment Fund (US Russia Foundation), Refugees International, and the San Francisco Film Festival Society. His legendary social skills were also in force in his role as owner of Slim's, a music club in San Francisco, which he started with musician Boz Scaggs.

"We were lucky to have Frank as an advisor," Fredrikson says. "He was described as 'he is like a god over here' by one of my former partners in the US, and he gave us excellent support, advice and global legitimacy throughout our development." Fredrikson points to one particular piece of advice that was followed by HealthCap's founding partners:

"I would highlight his insistence that we focus on what we were good at 'in order not to dilute our resources, results and reputation away from our core competencies'."

According to Odlander, Caufield's contribution and impact on HealthCap cannot be overestimated:

> "Frank was such a huge support – both in the early days and as the business evolved. He gave us a valuable perspective on the global venture capitalist world as we were shaping our business at the start, but he also gave valuable input as HealthCap grew and faced more complex challenges." He continues: "Frank was a friend as well as a business advisor, and he is sorely missed."

Good Ideas Don't Always Succeed

INVESTING IN LIFE science is risky, but if you don't try you may never be able to find products that can make it to the market. However, even if an idea doesn't make it into a product that can be used by patients, lessons are learnt. The scientific research that has been carried out can also lead to a better understanding of a disease area, which might prove to be important in future developments.

Eugen Steiner came to HealthCap in 1997 as a venture partner, and he's been with the company ever since.

"As you know, most things fail. We set up everything in the right way, but the technology doesn't pan out or the financing doesn't pan out. Deal windows close, technology goes out of favour or the data just doesn't show it will make a product. All of these things have happened to us in the 25 years," Steiner explains.

That's how Steiner views a portfolio company that was wound up when early experiments in targeting brain tumour cancer cells couldn't be replicated.

"Everything went to plan, on budget and on time but the experiments failed," he says. "The technology didn't pan out. We did one or two extra experiments just to be sure – but we could not repeat the results within the safety framework that was necessary. So, we closed down the company."

Failure for high-risk projects is part of everyday life for venture capitalists investing in the life science sector.

"It is not uncommon that experiments cannot be repeated," Steiner says. "In the cancer field there are numerous studies that show that while science can be very good, the models used are so specific and then when others try to repeat the experiments up to 80% fail."

He continues: "That doesn't necessarily mean the science is bad – it's just that it is not robust enough to become a product. But the science can still generate interesting data."

The company Glionova was formed following a discovery by scientists at the Karolinska Institutet in Stockholm. They had found a substance that seemed to explode cancer cells in brain tumours while normal cells remained intact. There is currently no cure for brain cancer and there has been little progress made since the first approvals in the mid-1990s of drugs to treat the disease. Any discovery in the area came with high potential – but also a high risk of failure.

To spread the risk HealthCap put together a small consortium consisting of themselves and two other VCs, Novo Holdings and Industrifonden. The funding was then topped up with some early grant money from the Swedish government.

Steiner was very enthused by the science but knew it was quite a leap in the dark:

> "This was, for me, the most fun and amazing project. The scientists were brilliant, they were very hard working. But it was very early and very risky, so we made strict rules for ourselves. We would test this and do the pre-clinical work, but if it didn't work, we would close it down. We had a predefined stop/go moment and so even though it is a bit of money down the drain it was actually a very low cost to the potential upside."

Patrik Ernfors, Professor of Tissue Biology at the Karolinska Institutet, was one of the driving forces behind the science at Glionova. Although the company did not end up with a product first time round, and was wound up, he says the data generated with HealthCap's support has benefitted scientific understanding of how to develop a drug for glioblastoma.

Glioblastoma is an aggressive type of cancer that can occur in the brain or spinal cord. It forms from cells called astrocytes that support nerve cells. Also known as glioblastoma multiforme, this cancer can be difficult to treat, and a cure is often not possible.

"The science was useful," Ernfors says. "We went back to basic science to learn more about mechanisms and treatment strategies. We now know much more about the compound. So, there is hope that there might be strategies for leveraging the effects of the compound so that it becomes clinically interesting."

Things can also not work out due to the financing needs of life science innovation. The development plans, regulatory frameworks and long timelines mean that a lot of capital is needed to bring ideas all the way through to the market. No matter how good the ideas are the macro-economic climate plays a huge role – that was clearly seen during the market crash at the turn of the century and also after the 9/11 terrorist attacks on the World Trade Center in New York in 2001 when risk appetites shrank.

This was also the case with Tengion, another of HealthCap's portfolio companies, which was founded in 2003 by three investors: HealthCap, the US VC Oak Investment Partners and J&J Development Corporation, the venture arm of the pharmaceutical company Johnson & Johnson.

Tengion focused on regenerative medicine, based on scientific research that damaged organs or tissues could be replaced by regenerated cells, which in turn could give patients with kidney, renal urologic or other disorders an alternative to transplantation.

As the innovation was based on cultivating autologous cells it was going to require a lot of capital. Carl-Johan Dalsgaard was the HealthCap partner responsible for Tengion:

> "To produce cells for clinical development and marketing you need to have a highly certified manufacturing facility known as a GMP facility – you cannot just order them up from a manufacturer somewhere in the world, as you can for a new chemical entity."

Dalsgaard, as well as having a career within the pharmaceutical industry, is an MD and specialist in plastic and reconstructive surgery. He joined HealthCap in 2000 as a venture partner and his experience with burns patients and skin regeneration gave him vital insight when working with Tengion:

> "So, it was a company with great ideas and was scientifically at the forefront, but by the time they came to try the cell regeneration idea out as a treatment for kidney organ damage there was a lack of support from the current investors and potential investors. It had just taken too long and had cost a lot of money."

Although the company ended up going bankrupt in 2014, the assets and tissue engineering samples were bought back by the creditors, including HealthCap and former executives of the company. HealthCap wanted to make sure that the science could be used to further build on knowledge in cell regeneration.

> "We could see the company didn't have the right support to be viable in the long term," Dalsgaard notes. "We brought the technology and the ongoing

study to Sweden to the Karolinska Institutet, where they had a cell manufacturing plant and could release the kidney cells and do the study properly. It was a controlled study, showing there was still merit to the technology."

Glionova and Tengion are good examples of the fact of business life that not all good ideas work. Many things need to be in place simultaneously to create a success – a promising market, support from the investment community, a well-structured development plan and an idea that can be proven to work within the framework for creating a viable product to name just a few.

The team at HealthCap is relatively philosophical about the fact that not everything they touch will turn to gold. Failure is part of the risk profile balancing act when HealthCap considers investment cases. The so-called "home runs", such as Algeta and Wilson Therapeutics, bring large returns on investments while other companies don't make it. New knowledge and understanding are, however, always gained.

From Underdog to Top Dog

IN THE LATE 2000S, HealthCap recruited Andrew Kay as the new CEO of Algeta, a Norwegian-based company in its portfolio that was focused on the treatment of prostate cancer. Kay had a long history of launching blockbusters for "big pharma" but had recently made the leap as an executive in biotech. HealthCap was looking for a heavyweight who could turn around the fortunes of Algeta and realise the potential it saw in the treatment and technology. With his strong commercial oncology background and experience in the pharmaceutical sector from positions in Renovo, Novartis, AstraZeneca and Eli Lilly, he was the perfect match. "HealthCap was a leading investor in Algeta but the company was running on ether and my role was to help refocus and make the story more attractive so we could raise more capital," Kay recalls.

> "The HealthCap team is a really smart group of people. Their philosophy is about bringing medicines to the market that provide real advantages to patients. I trusted them when they said 'look at the data, it's good', and I trusted them both to back me as the CEO and to back the company so that we could bring this product all the way through to market."

Founded in 1997, Algeta came onto HealthCap's radar screen reasonably quickly, but it wasn't until 2005 that it got involved by leading a consortium of investors, including Advent and SR One, raising a total of around EUR 23 million (around NOK 185 million) for injection into the company. HealthCap partner Johan Christenson recalls:

> "When we first looked at Algeta we did not fully agree on the strategy, but luckily enough the founders and existing management were open-minded, which allowed a creative discussion on future strategies. The company was

then focused on using radiopharmaceuticals as a palliative approach, to treat patients' pain. We believed instead the company should take a therapeutic approach and use radiopharmaceuticals to treat tumours, as the radiation has the potential to kill tumour cells."

Christenson explains how HealthCap supported Algeta in creating evidence on why their approach might work.

"We interacted with a leading doctor, a so-called key opinion leader, or KOL, at the Karolinska Institutet. Together, we analysed early patient data, which indicated a strong biological effect. This data convinced us about the therapeutic potential and triggered interest from SR One and Advent to join the syndicate."

The change of focus for the lead product Xofigo – from palliative care to cancer treatment – meant that in just two short years, after the 2005 private financing round led by HealthCap, Algeta was sufficiently attractive to public equity investors for it to be listed on the stock market in Oslo, raising USD 41 million. The successful recruitment of Kay followed four years later – and in 2013 Xofigo became the first marketed alpha-particle-emitting radiopharmaceutical following its approval in the US as a treatment for prostate cancer and a certain type of bone metastases, after a Phase 3 study that showed the product increased overall survival of patients with castration-resistant prostate cancer and symptomatic bone metastases by 2.8 months compared to patients in the placebo group.

Christenson continues:

"With Algeta we took the decision to invest and put in a new management team and worked as a sounding board for management to refocus the strategy. The process allowed us to create a shared vision with management – so it wasn't just about valuation, it was about the direction the company was going in. We did an IPO and evolved the management team again, ultimately leading to a two-stage deal with the pharmaceutical giant Bayer."

The Bayer deal was brokered under the leadership of Kay. After joining Algeta in 2009, one of his first tasks was to persuade others of the potential value of Xofigo and the Algeta approach. The result was a major deal announced later that year, between Algeta and Bayer for the development and commercialisation of Xofigo, worth USD 800 million. Christenson continues:

"Radiopharmaceuticals as a class of drugs had a really bad reputation. Our data was very good, but people wouldn't look at it because they were blinkered by their old image of radiopharmaceuticals. We got them to look at it again by talking about the product in terms of being an alpha pharmaceutical instead. CEO Kay insisted the whole Algeta organisation rebrand the product as the first-in-class alpha pharmaceutical with unique advantages in bone metastases. As the data was compelling it then became an open discussion and people began getting excited."

Algeta's venture capitalist shareholders wanted to get value on an exit, and in order to get a healthy return on their investment HealthCap and the management team at the company realised the need to build solid value by booking sales. Kay remembers the conversations with the board:

"In discussions about how to add value for an eventual deal with pharma, the board wanted to retain a massive geography outright, as they felt we could exit better on that. But, having launched many blockbusters, I knew the potential costs of doing that on our own could be enormous and that we would have a tough time selling the idea to future investors that they would need to fund such costs while we proved we could commercialise a product."

Instead, Kay chose another course of action:

"I said to the board, I want to do a deal with Bayer, a big licensing deal, but instead of keeping European geography we will keep half the US market and co-launch with Bayer in the US. We will use all of Bayer's strength and if we get the product to be big enough, we will get a big exit. It was seen by the board as a gutsy move, and this is where HealthCap was really good. They completely understood this approach – and supported it."

The Bayer deal gave Algeta the option to co-market Xofigo in the US, a huge task for a small European biotech. Algeta had begun the task of building up a world-class commercial force in the US and recognised it had to be as good as – if not better than – an entrenched Bayer salesforce in its home market. Kay describes HealthCap's support as invaluable in taking on such a bold task. Although these days it is usual for European-born biotech companies to develop organisations in the US and have the US market as a focus, a decade ago this was less common.

For Kay, HealthCap's underlying philosophy of trying to get much-needed products to patients meant that they all understood that being bold would create the best foundation for success in the US.

> "They realised that we needed to fully commit and invest in this launch, so we went out there and recruited great people – we paid top dollar but assembled a world-class team. From the appointment of Jeff Albers as Algeta US President through to the field force we had a philosophy of recruiting the very best people. We spent a lot of time on it, but we got big rewards in the end. We outsold Bayer in the US. Jeff and his team did a brilliant job of selling Xofigo."

Once Algeta had shown the market potential for the product in the US, Bayer offered to acquire Algeta in full for USD 2.9 billion. The deal, approved by HealthCap as the largest shareholder, was completed in March 2014 and was one of the largest deals in the pharmaceutical industry that year.

A focused strategy and a willingness to invest in order to build value are key elements of growing a company to achieve success in the business of delivering products to patients. But Kay is philosophical that you also need a bit of karma or luck in biotech.

> "When I joined Algeta we always used to do our quarterly briefings in this strange building in the centre of Oslo, with high ceilings and very dark interiors. It had really strange karma – a strange atmosphere for me anyway. And we always did our briefings on a Friday and the next quarterly meeting was on Friday 13th. I'm not superstitious, but I said that we will never use this building again and we will never do briefings on a Friday again."

Kay continues:

> "They all thought this was a bit of a strange decision. We moved our earnings briefings down the road to what I felt was a much better and more prestigious building with a welcoming atmosphere, and our luck changed. However, the most important factor – true for all biotechs – was we had an incredibly strong and experienced senior management team who all believed in the product and worked day and night to deliver Xofigo as a major success. They were the key to this success story."

Knowledge Adds Value

> "In my early career as part of my training I ended up at a hospital in the Bronx, New York, where there were two world experts in Wilson Disease. One patient died of liver disease without a diagnosis – but if he had been diagnosed and could then have been treated there might have been a different outcome. I guess that stayed on my conscience and drove my future focus."

MICHAEL SCHILSKY REFERS to a moment he will never forget. Dr Schilsky has been the Medical Director of Adult Liver Transplant at Yale New Haven Transplantation Center since 2007. He is also an internationally recognised expert in Wilson Disease, a rare genetic disorder in which excessive amounts of copper accumulate in the body – a condition that affects around 1 in 30,000 people globally.

Like Schilsky, HealthCap became interested in Wilson Disease, but its interest was piqued by a particular scientific innovation that it believed could be a potential treatment for patients with this rare disease. That interest resulted in the creation of strong networks and an immense knowledge bank in the field of Wilson Disease, and has led to further investments in the field. HealthCap partner Mårten Steen explains:

> "We started the company Wilson Therapeutics to develop a product that really looked like something that could help patients suffering from Wilson Disease. We learnt so much about this disease that when we found further innovations in the area, we were comfortable in seed financing yet another company, Spanish-French Vivet Therapeutics."

According to Schilsky one of the key issues for rare diseases is to diagnose them.

"We really have to look for these diseases as the cause of symptoms, as a lack of diagnosis can be devastating and have irreversible effects," Schilsky says. "One of the challenges of Wilson Disease is that it has a depth and breadth of presence that few other diseases have. It needs a multidisciplinary approach as it has many different presentations."

"We believe it is essential to bring the academic, scientific and business communities together to succeed in developing products that solve unmet medical needs within rare diseases," says HealthCap's Björn Odlander.

Schilsky describes the advantages of working with HealthCap:

"There was always a human element to the development – was this meaningful and is this helpful for treating the disease? It's never perfect forming partnerships across the corporate and medical divide but here the collaboration added a lot. The study built in a multidisciplinary focus, gathering the Wilson Disease community together, and ensured a broad focus in the future on the disease."

Schilsky welcomes HealthCap's focus on patients' needs:

"There has been a lack of enthusiasm for research development for treatments of rare diseases from traditional funding sources in industry. But in HealthCap, here was a company that was interested in the disease and wanted to partner with us. We were intellectual partners for the development without getting caught in the financial complications that might sink a rare disease," Schilsky says.

Another area of expertise built up within HealthCap is that of radiopharmaceuticals. This type of drug emits radiation and therefore has the potential to be used as a precision medicine targeting and killing cancer cells. HealthCap has invested in a number of companies developing radiopharmaceutical products and was, as discussed in the previous chapter, the leading investor in Algeta, arguably one of the most successful Nordic biotech companies, which was sold to Bayer in 2014 for USD 2.9 billion. HealthCap also counts Nordic Nanovector, Precirix, Ariceum and Fusion Pharmaceuticals as portfolio companies, all of which specialise in radiopharmaceuticals.

HealthCap's interest in radiopharmaceuticals began at the start of the millennium when looking at Algeta's lead product. As HealthCap partner Dr Johan Christenson explains: "The team believed there was huge potential in the idea of creating drugs that contain radioactive isotopes to be used in treatment and diagnosis. At the time, Algeta was focused on using its lead product for palliative care but HealthCap was convinced therapeutic use would create more value."

In 1997, Dr Roy Larsen, based in Oslo, Norway, and a nuclear chemist by background, was one of the scientific founders of the company that eventually became Algeta. Larsen left Algeta in 2006, to again pursue his passion of turning research projects into clinical projects, and he sees HealthCap's role in supporting early development as essential:

> "With Algeta, HealthCap came on board in 2005. They were very valuable for the company as they had skills in how to finance this kind of business. They also have good networks within the VC community and brought in another strong investor, Abingworth from the UK, getting international interest in the technology."

Larsen also points to HealthCap's role in the Nordic community as important in highlighting the scientific work being done there: "Their expertise in understanding the radiopharmaceuticals landscape has helped them identify interesting projects and helped to turn research into product development."

"HealthCap has been important in highlighting the possibility of biotech in Norway," Larsen stresses. "They were behind and supported the first really successful biotech company in Norway – Algeta – and they have supported Nordic Nanovector. Their understanding of the science is important as it spotlights good science."

For Odlander, the creation of knowledge centres of excellence around disease areas and drug classes is a welcome by-product of HealthCap's 25 years in the life science sector. Thus, HealthCap's impact has led not only to products reaching patients, but also to the enrichment of the scientific landscape and to partnerships created between industry and academia. Odlander says:

> "I'm really proud that academics see the value of working with us, and we truly see the value of collaborating with the medical and scientific research communities. We can turn projects into meaningful medicines that can benefit patients, and that is ultimately our mission. We work hard to do good, and we can only do that by working with all the different people who provide a multitude of aspects on life science innovation."

How to Exit – and When?

VENTURE CAPITALISTS ALWAYS have to exit their investments at some point, and choosing that point can be challenging, both from a business and personal perspective. To date HealthCap has made 96 exits from portfolio companies. As HealthCap partner Eugen Steiner puts it:

> "It's always hard to exit the portfolio companies we have invested in – we know we have to do it, but you always fall a little bit in love with your projects."

Sometimes, further investment is needed to get the best out of an investment. In order to secure the best return on their investment, venture capitalists (VCs) want to build as much value as possible in a company – and with drug or medical device development this can take time and a lot of funding. Therefore, it is not unusual for VCs to want to further the company, by raising public equity via an initial public offering (IPO) to list on a stock market. An IPO can either create an exit for a VC fund, where they realise their investment, or it can be used to ensure additional funding to continue building value in the firm for a later exit.

The discussion on the next steps for any company was one that took place during 2018 and 2019 between the Board of Directors and management at Pulmonx.

Pulmonx is a commercial stage medical technology company that provides solutions to treat patients with severe emphysema, a form of chronic obstructive pulmonary disease (COPD). The company has an approved product, the Zephyr valve, which can be fitted with minimally invasive surgery, to reduce hyperinflation associated with severe emphysema. The valve is a breakthrough technology, has pre-market approval by the FDA and has been used by more than 20,000 patients globally.

The overwhelming support and advice from the investment banking community was that Pulmonx would be a very attractive candidate for the public markets. A Strategic IPO Committee was set up, chaired by HealthCap partner and Pulmonx Board of Directors' member Staffan Lindstrand, to prepare for an eventual listing. During this time, the company received several unsolicited approaches for a private buyout, which prompted many deep discussions on the best way forward. Should there be an IPO to further grow the company or a trade sale that would lead to all the current investors realising their investment?

"I have done many IPOs, but as usual everyone is in a new situation and I learnt a lot from doing this one," Lindstrand says. "It was a US listing, and the considerations are slightly different in the US when looking to list a company."

According to Lindstrand, in Europe, generally, one of the biggest issues to be aware of when discussing an IPO is protecting existing shareholders, meaning that dilution is a very sensitive topic. Whereas in the US, there are other considerations that are equally, if not more, important, such as what's in the best long-term interest of the company rather than the maybe shorter-term view for existing shareholders, in particular regarding smaller minority investors. He explains:

> "The priorities are to find capital and to ensure there is a sustainable market after the IPO, enabling good share price development. You need to ensure there is free float enough – the number of shares available to be bought and sold on a daily basis – so there is good trading afterwards. In the end it's the value of your holding that's of importance and not the ownership percentage."

The IPO was slated for March 2020 and many pre-roadshow meetings were held with positive feedback. The arrival of the COVID-19 pandemic, however, resulting in huge operational uncertainty, looked as if it might ruin the plans that everyone at the company and in the investment banking syndicate had been working on. As it turned out, after the initial rollercoaster reaction, the markets regained buoyancy relatively quickly after the second quarter of the year.

There was immense investor interest in the Pulmonx story, which, according to Lindstrand, was due to the first-in-class nature of the case and the strong fundamentals of the business, which compared well to other successful med-tech companies. Lindstrand also believes that the appetite for buying a stake in Pulmonx was strong because the med-tech sector has recently enjoyed success:

"We had all the things in place that make an IPO in this sector compelling. There was good potential in terms of the total addressable market, the revenue growth rate and the gross margins. Pulmonx ticked all the boxes as a great first-in-class story."

The senior management team, led by CEO Glen French, were also impressive at explaining the story and the potential value to investors.

"In the end," Lindstrand continues, "it turned out that the pause due to COVID-19 was not entirely bad. Investors had more time to get to know the story and the management team as they carried out meetings with investors – which increased credibility. The pandemic also meant the IPO process was extremely efficient – with more virtual meetings with investors over a four-day period than they would have done if they had carried out the traditional two weeks of physical roadshow meetings."

The IPO was fixed for late September and from an initial size of USD 100 million, with a price range of USD 14–16 per share, the pressure from interested investors meant the deal size was upped, with both a higher price range of USD 17–18 per share as well as an increase in the number of shares being offered for sale.

When the transaction closed, the offering had generated over USD 4.1 billion in demand from investors who wanted stock, resulting in a final price of a dollar above the second range and three dollars above the original published range at USD 19. Ten million shares were sold, and the investment bank consortium also exercised its greenshoe option (giving an extra allocation of 1.5 million shares), which made the total deal size, including the extra shares, almost USD 220 million.

"We were very happy with the IPO," Lindstrand says. "Around 98% of investors having one-on-one virtual meetings submitted offers to buy shares, and it was nice to see that all investors we felt would be beneficial as holders of the stock came into the deal."

Even though the pathway to the IPO had been challenging, Pulmonx's story and the value created in the company by the strategy executed by management underlines the compelling story for investors on the public markets.

As Bruno Stembaum, from Bank of America, stated at the time of the IPO: "Pulmonx was one of the most successful med-tech IPOs in the last decade as the company was perceived as a 'must-own' stock by every investor of consequence in the healthcare space."

ACT FOR
FACTS

Excitement, Experience and Precision

"THE COMMON FACTS of today are the result of yesterday's research," said Australian politician Duncan MacDonald (1885–1977).

The innovations that HealthCap invests in are built on such research, where scientists have delved into the data and hypotheses and developed new, creative potential solutions.

From the very beginning, HealthCap believed in turning scientific research into medicines or products to help patients. Today, the members of the team are constantly sifting through scientific research to find innovations in life science.

As the company has grown, the strategy too has developed. HealthCap has become more focused on adding value to innovations by providing skill sets across a broad range of areas including scientific, regulatory, financial and commercial landscapes in the life science sector.

Partner Staffan Lindström joined HealthCap in 1997, a year after inception, when the net for ideas was cast quite broadly.

"There was more serendipity then," he says. "In the early days we were looking at a lot of things and would often find interesting innovative ideas that we felt could have potential."

As is normal in a start-up, in the early days of HealthCap there was an atmosphere of excitement – of trying out different things that you believe will work. A quarter-century later, there is still excitement about innovations but there are also many years of experience of investing in the life science sector to draw upon and that is evident round the table during the partner group's weekly Monday meetings.

HealthCap's mission is to create value, both in terms of investors in the funds and the end user – the patient or consumer. As well as a return on investment, the team looks at the potential to establish and grow interesting workplaces and jobs, with employees who pay taxes to the state and the region, with a strong desire to develop meaningful new medicines or devices for people.

According to partner Per Samuelsson, HealthCap's model is based on the US model of venture capital only in terms of value creation, because the company has brought its own Nordic value set to the culture as well as working structures to build success.

"We have a consensus decision-making model," Samuelsson explains. "We discuss a lot and take on board the different experiences we have around the partner table. It is not like a traditional model where VC partners often fight for resources and get rewarded based on their individual deals."

At HealthCap partners work in pairs, with one science and one business partner, so that multiple skill sets are brought to portfolio companies. Samuelsson continues:

> "Our model with two partners for each portfolio company means we can do very thorough due diligence and can challenge each other on theories and assumptions. It's a very healthy and enjoyable way to work and rather unique in my opinion!"

HealthCap's ability to collaborate is also an important factor in determining how the VC secures the creation of value in businesses. Timelines are traditionally lengthy in the life science sector, with many developmental and regulatory hurdles before products can reach the market. To accommodate this, HealthCap creates syndicates to ensure innovation is well funded and portfolio companies have enough resources to build solid sustainable businesses.

From the outset the VC was different in this way from traditional Swedish investors, using insight and experience to be an active investor, supporting strategy, the recruitment of talented teams with international experience and focused operations.

"Previously the situation in Sweden was that investors were local and quite passive, often lacking life science industry experience," Samuelsson recalls. "We have a team of professionals who are very experienced in the life science sector and understand the risk–reward profile. The VC group brings power to support companies."

Samuelsson goes on: "Our horizon to build companies has a strict time limit of around ten–twelve years – and our aim is to be globally relevant, to build the companies that are best in the world not just the best in Sweden or the Nordics."

Forming syndicates is key not only to ensuring HealthCap can remain relevant, but also to continue to control its own destiny by not growing too large. Dr Carl Kilander was promoted to partner at HealthCap in 2021. He says building syndicates helps to tackle the challenge of fund size:

> "We want to be relevant and take meaningful stakes, but we really don't want to be too large with too much capital to deploy so we are forced to take mega stakes that limit our and the company's options as we become less flexible."

Healthcare innovation and drug development is a risky venture, and it is important to learn from past experience and apply that to future investments:

> "We like to invest early and be part of the company building, and we really believe in our precision medicine investment strategy. This investment strategy has evolved over many years of investing. It is centred around focusing on the right medicine for the right patient and having more precise treatments for patients based on good understanding of the underlying disease biology."

A key strength in HealthCap's success and accompanying longevity is to be adaptive and learn from past experiences. According to HealthCap partner Mårten Steen, the focus on precision medicine has developed organically from the pursuit of providing innovative solutions to unmet medical needs and being patient-centric.

"Precision medicine was not a deliberate focus at the start of HealthCap, but we have learnt over time that this strategy reduces failure rates and accelerates timelines and generates better performance in the end," Steen concludes.

Breaking Advanced Frontiers

THROUGHOUT ITS 25-YEAR history, HealthCap has maintained a passion for identifying innovative ideas and investing in people and companies developing new and potentially groundbreaking products, which make a truly meaningful difference for patients.

During this time, the healthcare sector has experienced remarkable evolution as the industry adapts to, and makes use of, new scientific breakthroughs to tackle previously difficult or impossible to treat diseases, or newly discovered and emerging challenges.

Recent advancements in cutting-edge biological therapies have led to a shift away from the traditional "one-size-fits-all" approach towards precision medicines which tailor medical treatments to individual patients' specific disease characteristics. The introduction of advanced cell- and gene-based products have opened new routes for the treatment of various types of cancers and incurable diseases. These new approaches target the underlying cause of diseases by correcting mutations, replacing defective cells or even reprogramming the immune system to fight diseases.

These types of drugs, which include novel tissue-engineered products and cell therapy and gene therapy, are grouped together under the term Advanced Therapy Medicinal Products (ATMPs). All classes of ATMP contain either living cells or viral vectors and have a high degree of complexity. Tissue-engineered products contain modified cells or tissues and are used to treat patients needing to regenerate, repair or replace human tissue. For example, in cell therapy the cells used usually come from the patient or a relevant donor and are processed, to be expanded and/or genetically engineered, in the laboratory before being re-administered to the patient in a hospital. Gene therapy is designed to introduce genetic material into living cells to compensate for defective genes and to express functional proteins.

Over the years HealthCap has backed several companies focused on gene therapy and cell therapy, including NeuroNova, Tengion, Targovax, Ultragenyx, GenSight, Vivet, Carisma and Mahzi Therapeutics. HealthCap partner Mårten Steen says:

> "We have been fortunate to work with ATMPs through our cell- and gene-therapy focused companies for many years and are thrilled to see how these companies are pioneers in the field of precision medicine. It is fascinating to follow how quickly the field is evolving."

The concept of gene therapy was suggested in the late 1970s after the introduction of recombinant DNA technology. After the development of the basic science and technology for gene transfer into patients' cells, the first gene therapy trial on humans was performed in 1990. Gene therapy technologies have continued to develop, allowing improvements in treatment as well as more precise delivery into tissues. Gene therapy has now been extensively tested in clinical trials where it has shown promise in treating a variety of diseases and resulted in a few new drug approvals, and HealthCap is at the cutting edge of investing in new innovations in this area.

Early on, gene therapy was explored within ophthalmology to try to treat inherited forms of blindness. The eye is easy to access and benefits from its ability to tolerate the introduction of antigens without triggering an immune response – the eye is therefore known as being immune-privileged. One of the pioneers in this field is Dr Jean Bennett, a founder of the HealthCap company GenSight Biologics. GenSight develops gene therapies for two inherited forms of blindness – Leber's Hereditary Optic Neuropathy (LHON) and Retinitis Pigmentosa (RP) – and is currently in late-stage clinical development with its lead programme for LHON.

Another of HealthCap's gene therapy ventures is Spanish-French gene therapy company Vivet Therapeutics, a spin-out from the University of Navarra in Spain. HealthCap was a founding investor together with Novartis Venture Fund and Columbus Venture Partners. Vivet is developing gene therapy products for liver-derived monogenic disorders such as Wilson Disease, Familiar Intrahepatic Cholestasis (PFIC) and Citrullinemia Type 1 (CTLN 1).

Ultragenyx is another company with a growing gene therapy pipeline. It is profiled in a separate chapter of this book, and has also developed a proprietary manufacturing technology using the oldest and most used immortal cell line in scientific research, HeLa cells.

RNA-based medicines is another fast-growing field of drug development. RNA, or ribonucleic acid, is a class of molecules involved in various biological roles in gene expression and regulation. Several RNA-based medicines have now been approved and the RNA medicine field is currently comprised of three different drug classes: antisense, RNA interference (RNAi) and RNA-based vaccines. The latter was, of course, the basis technology for the rapidly developed first approved COVID-19 vaccine in the US and Europe at the end of 2020.

Antisense and RNAi are based on decreasing disease-causing protein in a highly specific manner, whereas RNA-based vaccines are based on evoking an immune response to viral proteins. One of HealthCap's recent investments was made in Aro Biotherapeutics. Aro is working with its proprietary centyrin platform to develop tissue-targeted delivery of RNA-based medicines. So far, a common challenge across RNA-based therapeutics has been the inability to selectively target these therapies to diseased tissues.

Another ATMP modality that has developed quickly over the last decade within the field of oncology is CAR-T cell therapy, where certain lymphocytic immune cells, called T-cells, are reprogrammed. By engineering the T-cells to express CAR, a tumour-recognising receptor, the T-cells can be targeted to leukaemic cancer cells. The CAR-T technology has been very effective in treating certain severe leukaemias, but success in using the technology to treat solid tumours has, so far, been more elusive.

HealthCap's Carisma Therapeutics is pioneering in the field of using the CAR technology to reprogramme another form of immune cells, macrophages, to tackle solid tumours. Macrophages are naturally drawn to solid tumours and have an ability to survive in the hostile solid tumour microenvironment.

The CAR macrophage technology is based on the work from two pioneers in the CAR field, Dr Saar Gill and Dr Carl June from the University of Pennsylvania. HealthCap was one of the founding investors, together with the venture arm of the pharmaceutical company AbbVie, in 2017. Carisma has made great progress since then and recently raised a second financing round of USD 59 million and has now, for the first time in history, treated patients with engineered macrophages.

Recently, Carisma entered into a strategic collaboration with Moderna Inc., bringing significant cash upfront and future milestone payments, aiming to further explore the CAR macrophage technology for the treatment of cancer. It is still early days for ATMPs and genetic medicine, with only a few therapies of this type approved so far. However, there is much excitement about the potential of the constantly evolving field, with multiple therapies in development which are hoped to reach the market in the foreseeable future. Regulators have also had to adapt to the changing landscape with these new types of product, and both the EU regulator EMA and the FDA in the US have put in place guidelines facilitating review processes to work with industry and academia to bring ATMP medicines to patients in need.

Due to the significant therapeutic potential of ATMPs for the treatment of serious conditions, their market share is anticipated to increase. One challenge is the high cost associated with ATMP products due to factors including expensive manufacturing, complex quality-control testing, expensive raw materials and cold chains being required for transfer. However, many of these treatments offer patients a potential cure to severe and deadly diseases, and in some cases with just a single intervention. The cost of treatment therefore needs to be weighed up in the light of the game-changing nature of the drugs when discussing pricing, affordability and the value they can bring to healthcare systems.

All this early innovation can lead to breakthroughs in the way we treat disease, but Steen also recognises that there is a long road ahead when developing pioneering therapeutics:

> "There are still many stones to turn to find new treatments for patients suffering from severe diseases. We also need to improve targeting of these new drug modalities to reach the right tissues and we must further understand the durability of these medicines and the need for re-dosing."

He continues:

> "So far results from ongoing clinical trials suggest that the durability can last for many years, but we are still on a learning curve. HealthCap believes that in the next 25 years this field will really take off and we are excited to be part of that journey."

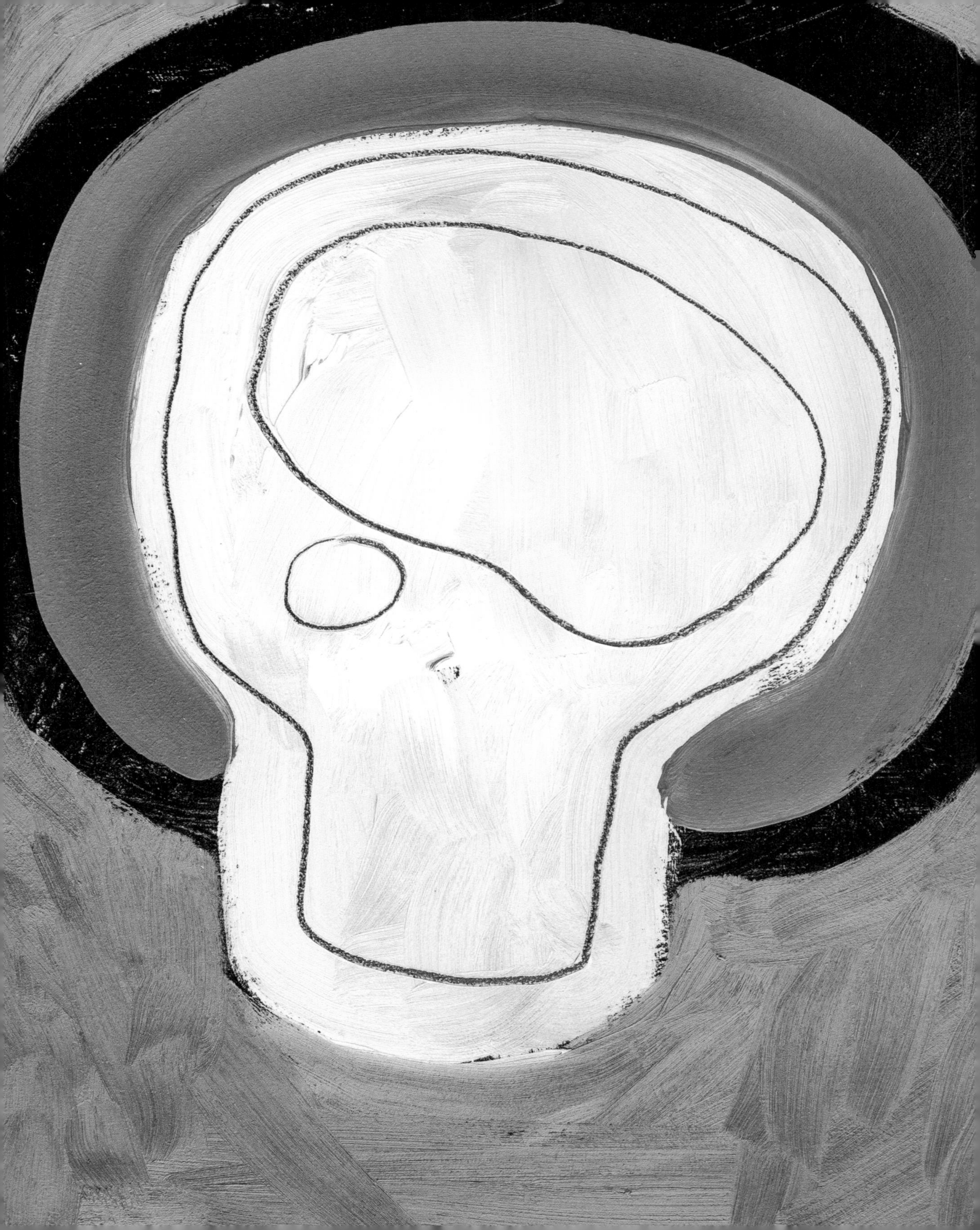

Don’t Lose Your Head

CHOOSING A HELMET for motorbike riders, cyclists, skiers or equestrians ought to be about safety, but, hands up, how many of us have also been swayed by design, colour and, of course, comfort? That was one of the surprising challenges when HealthCap invested in a seemingly obvious innovation – safer helmets that better protect the brain during sports, work and leisure activities. Manufacturers took a lot of persuasion to understand that better safety could be a compelling selling point for consumers.

HealthCap discovered the innovation behind the helmet technology MIPS during a routine scouting trip to a meeting held at Sweden’s Royal Institute of Technology (KTH). MIPS stands for “Multidirectional Impact Protection System” and does what it says in the name – it is a technology that makes helmets safer, by protecting the brain more effectively against trauma.

MIPS was developed back in the 1990s when the Swedish neurosurgeon Professor Hans von Holst, who was working at the Karolinska Institutet in Stockholm, was convinced that helmets could be improved to better protect against brain injuries. A student at KTH at the time, Peter Halldin, carried out research on the biomechanics of injuries to the head and neck, and in 1996 the two men presented their idea for the MIPS solution, a technology to be used in helmet design. Professor von Holst worked at the Karolinska Institutet until 2014 and Halldin subsequently built his career at MIPS, as the company is known, and is today Chief Science Officer in the business.

The MIPS technology consists of sliding layers inserted into a helmet and these absorb rotational energy on impact. Traditionally, helmets were designed to protect the head from skull fractures caused by a one-directional force of impact. The MIPS technology builds on the understanding that the most common severe brain injuries, such as diffuse axonal injury and subdural haematoma, occur more easily when the head is subjected to rotational motion. The idea behind MIPS was to try and protect the brain from damage when subjected to an angled impact.

Jacob Gunterberg, then partner at HealthCap, explains:

"In a way, the underlying need for safer helmets was created by this invention, as before MIPS came along no one was interested in making safer helmets. We were naive and thought this would be a very straightforward idea for helmet-maker brands. But the helmet-makers asked us 'why should we buy something from you that makes our helmets more expensive? No one is asking for that. All people want is comfort, ventilation – and design.'"

For HealthCap though, the idea was compelling. It did not fit directly with the core focus of investing in therapies for the treatment of severe diseases, but the team liked the science and concept behind MIPS and really believed it was an innovation that should reach consumers. This meant a different way of working.

"So, we decided to keep the investment on the low side," Gunterberg explains, "but devote even more time and work to see if it would be possible to develop a market for this new and potentially life-saving technology. It was an investment with our hearts. We believed in this idea and, initially, I was involved in everything from nitty-gritty details to activities such as talking to customers and suppliers as well as visiting fairs and looking at office premises."

HealthCap's involvement began in 2008 when MIPS was in dire need of capital and on the verge of bankruptcy. At the time MIPS was marketing proprietary and MIPS-branded equestrian helmets in Sweden, but due to a quality issue it had been forced to carry out a large product recall. As well as providing lifeline funding by becoming the leading and largest shareholder, HealthCap supported the business by helping to recruit new management and by developing a new business plan.

"The founders of MIPS were not skilled business people," remembers Björn Odlander. "As a new investor, HealthCap could help with bringing different skill sets to running a business, bringing in management and a new focus to strategy."

Rather than marketing a MIPS-branded helmet, the business model was refocused to market the technology to other branded helmet-makers across a range of sectors – skiing, cycling, motocross and many more. Although it took time to persuade helmet manufacturers of the value of a technology which added safety features that were not visible to the customer, by 2014 15 helmet-maker brands had started to sell helmets equipped with MIPS technology.

A breakthrough then occurred when the world's largest helmet manufacturer at the time, BRG Sports, Inc., under the Giro and Bell brands, alongside a few other larger brands, decided to implement MIPS in some of its models. BRG also invested in MIPS, becoming a significant shareholder.

"The CEO at BRG, who had originally been the founder of the company, asked his employees to drop any 'not invented here' thoughts and instead look at what MIPS offered," Gunterberg explains. "His R&D people told him that there was something interesting in the MIPS technology."

In 2015, more than a million helmets were sold across 28 brands with the MIPS technology. MIPS debuted on the Stockholm Nasdaq main market in 2017. HealthCap traded out of its position carefully over time.

Gunterberg views the investment as having had a significant impact on the helmet market: "All helmets are still certified in the same way, with the same tests – so helmets have a safety certification, but the MIPS technology makes them much better, adding an extra, important layer of safety for the user."

Today, with over 15 million helmets containing the technology having been sold worldwide, MIPS is one of the most celebrated technology spin-outs from KTH. With a market cap at the end of 2021 of around SEK 32 billion (approximately USD 3.5 billion) and net sales in 2021 reaching SEK 608 million (approximately USD 64 million), HealthCap is understandably proud of the success of the company. The MIPS story also encapsulates HealthCap's strategy of funding innovation to solve important medical needs, in this case from a preventive perspective. The technology offers safer helmets to consumers across the globe, and in many different sectors, and will hopefully minimise the number of brain injuries from trauma. At the same time, HealthCap has nurtured a company providing jobs and income to society as well as returns for their investors.

And with MIPS technology now used by many global brands design and colour are no longer contradictory to safety.

A Rare Company for Ultra-Rare Disorders

"I was at HealthCap's annual CEO gathering near Stockholm a few years ago – every year they invite the leaders of their portfolio companies to come and meet each other and swap experiences and learnings. I was able to go that year, and it was such a great, diverse group of people. HealthCap is bold and their successes have shown their philosophy is proved right. They are doing good things, and these were people I wanted to work with."

THIS IS THE sentiment from Emil Kakkis, the CEO of Ultragenyx, one of HealthCap's portfolio companies. Ultragenyx brings novel therapies to patients with rare and ultra-rare diseases, with a focus on serious, debilitating genetic diseases. A medical geneticist with an MD and PhD from the UCLA Medical Scientist programme, Kakkis has spent his career developing treatments for ultra-rare disorders but had not considered setting up a company himself. All that changed in 2010.

"So many parents were calling me to ask me to help them by developing treatments for their kids. I realised there was more to do in this area, and I needed to create a new company to work on rare and also on ultra-rare diseases."

Driven very much by purpose, Kakkis' idea was to speed up development times while keeping patient needs and safety in focus.

"We were committed to devising smarter, faster and more efficient development strategies – but also with the right level of compassion, so we achieved both a good business and patient outcome," Kakkis says, speaking from his company office in California. "After the first year of getting two products in the pipeline I then focused on getting venture funding, and it was here I met HealthCap."

HealthCap joined three other investors in a financing round known as a Series A in June 2011, raising a total of USD 30 million, much to Kakkis' delight: "I had been looking for investors that were bold and creative and doing informative things, not just people trying to flip money. From their investments I could see HealthCap was working on real companies trying to do transformative type of work."

Kakkis made the trip from California to Stockholm in spring 2011 and got a good feeling about the team: "They were medically trained, very deep on science, it was about the mission and not just about the money. For me that is very important."

Because the goal of a venture capitalist (VC) is to build value in companies to attract further funding at a higher valuation later on, HealthCap partner Mårten Steen joined the Ultragenyx Board of Directors and supported Kakkis' vision of how to broaden the pipeline and build further value.

"With Mårten's support we could add a third programme to our development activities, despite this adding more cash burn, but it helped us do a crossover investment later on, in 2012, where we raised an additional USD 75 million," Kakkis says and continues:

> "We'd only used around USD 15 million at that point, so after that fund raise we had over USD 90 million in the bank, which is pretty good funding for an early-stage company. This allowed us to negotiate a deal to add a fourth product to the pipeline, as the Japanese company we were dealing with felt more comfortable that we had a strong financial base."

With five programmes from four products in clinical development at the end of 2013, Ultragenyx was able to go public in January 2014 with a valuation of more than USD 1 billion on the first trading day.

Today, the company has around 800 employees, and during the first year after its founding Kakkis interviewed every single employee to ensure they were in line with his ideas on company culture and had the patients' needs in focus. Some ten years on he still interviews all potential employees at VP level or above:

> "Our organisation is about being connected to patients. We hold an annual family day at our headquarters in Novato, California, where we bring a couple of hundred patients and their families and our employees and their families to meet each other – so people working in our *rare company* get to meet *rare families* and understand them."

Kakkis has been active for decades in working to influence policy decisions in the area of rare diseases. The year before he started Ultragenyx, he founded the EveryLife Foundation for Rare Diseases, a non-profit organisation aimed at accelerating biotech innovation for rare diseases. It is this focus on providing new options for patients with rare or ultra-rare diseases that drives him, and he is keen to stress that at Ultragenyx purpose always comes first. In his view, HealthCap understands and supports this spirit, and this is what makes it impactful.

> "To put a team together to take millions of dollars and turn them into treatments you have to be on the same page in terms of the philosophy and in your approach and be dedicated to the purpose. When you chase the money, it glides away, but when you build something of value the money will come to you. I think HealthCap really get that."

More companies have started to focus on treatments for rare diseases during the last ten years or so. However, Kakkis is not worried that the area might become more competitive:

> "There are 7,000 rare diseases and 95% don't have a treatment. So, there is still a lot of room. I look at any competition as giving patients the best shot of an answer. Our goal is not to copy people but foraging in the areas that are undiscovered and finding treatments for things that people aren't paying attention to."

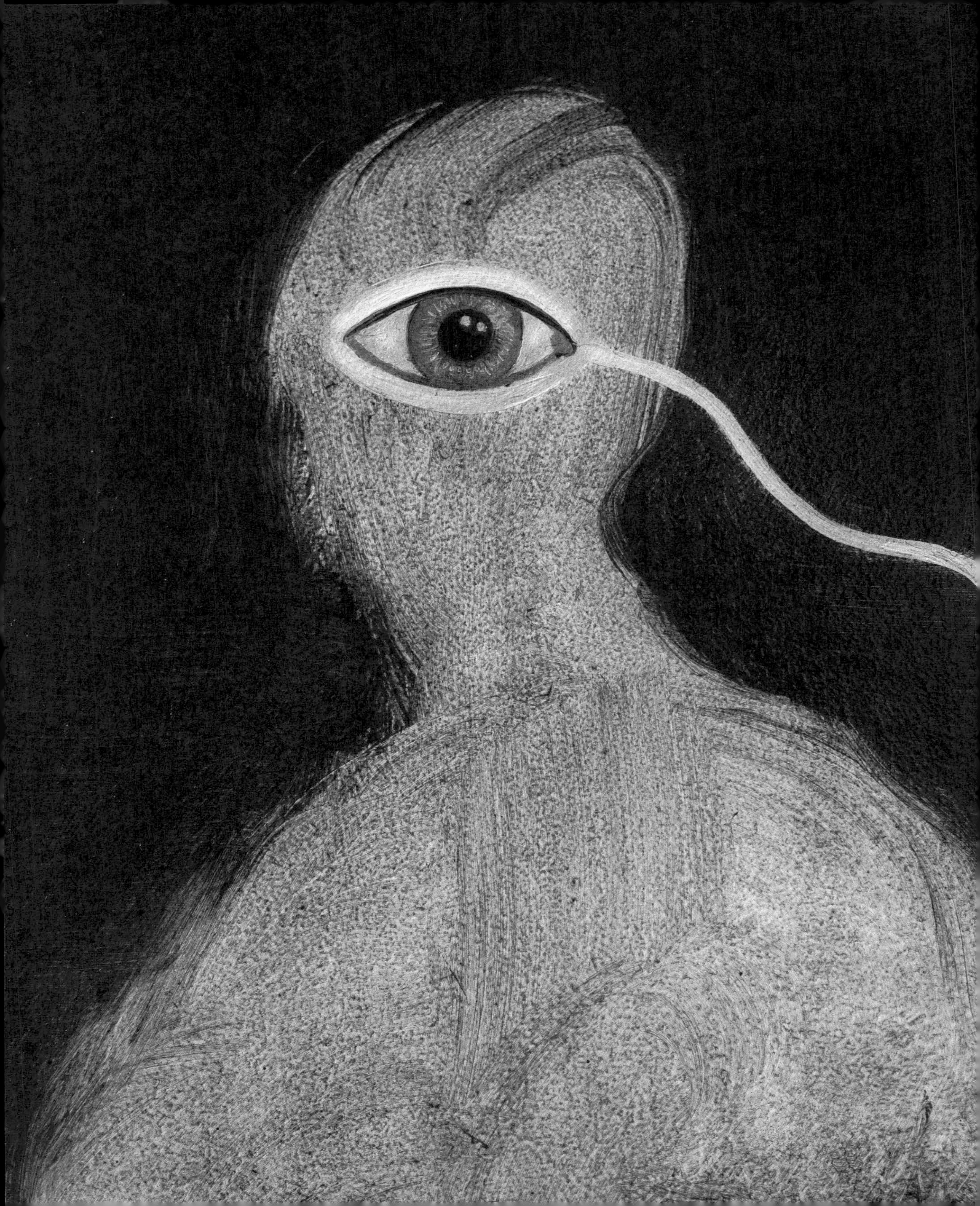

Stronger Together – a View from a Fellow Investor

"IF YOU WANT growth in your society, risk capital and knowledgeable risk capital is key."

So says Søren Møller, managing partner of Novo Seeds, a life science-focused venture fund within Novo Holdings, which is the asset management arm of the Novo Nordisk Foundation.

Like HealthCap, Novo Seeds is committed to supporting innovation in the Nordic region by building companies that can play on the global stage while creating value in the Nordics from their start-up roots. It is typically an early investor in young companies where founders need financial support and help in how to build a business from a scientific innovation. Sitting in the Novo Holdings' office on the harbour front in Copenhagen, Møller explains:

> "We are focused on the same thing. Both HealthCap and Novo Seeds are looking for how we can support innovations that answer a need in the market. We have networks of talented, experienced people and can help establish start-ups so they can turn ideas into viable products."

A mere youngster compared to HealthCap, Novo Seeds was founded in 2007 in Denmark with the goal of tapping into the rich pool of scientific expertise in the Nordics and turning innovative ideas from the academic environment into products to be developed by start-ups and early-stage development companies. During the last few years, the impact of venture capital (VC) has been influential in creating a blossoming biotech ecosystem in Denmark, Sweden and Norway.

In 2021, Novo Seeds portfolio companies have raised a record DKK 3.6 billion (around USD 550 million) in funding from international VCs and the investor has led three of the largest Series A financings in Europe. At the time of print the group had

36 portfolio companies, having evaluated over 2000 projects and companies since foundation in 2007. Novo Seeds aims to invest around DKK 700 million (or around USD 110 million) each year, primarily in companies in the Nordic region.

Møller has a PhD in molecular biology and was a postdoc at Stanford Medical School. Having worked in international biotech companies before joining Novo Seeds, he was acutely aware of the need to partner the top-class scientific know-how in the region with development and business acumen. Both HealthCap and Novo Seeds take a long-term view of building value into companies. A side effect of this longevity is the build-up of competencies in the region.

> "In the last few years, VC investment in the Nordic life science sector has enabled a tremendous development in creating a pool of experienced management here. Now we have repeat entrepreneurs that have done it before and have strong networks in industry as well as academia," Møller says. "And we are also getting off the curve with capital. Today, we can build a syndicate with EUR 30 million that can be invested in life science start-ups, and that requires good management, good science and a plan."

HealthCap truly values the growth in the VC life science sector in the Nordic region, believing it enables both better financing and stronger companies built on interesting innovations. Møller is also keen to ensure that innovative ideas are not left languishing in the world of academia but can instead be developed with the potential to end as novel healthcare solutions:

> "Venture-backed companies supply pharma with more than half of the innovation that goes on to become new, approved drugs, so it is a proven model. You need specialist investors because it is such a complex and knowledge-heavy industry – regulatory, data, science and financial know-how is essential."

Both HealthCap and Novo Seeds see themselves as important enablers for life science innovators in the Nordic region to be in a position to pursue a global agenda. Møller believes the sector can only benefit by having strong European VCs:

> "Having partners such as HealthCap, who have the international mindset, the networks and the knowledge to judge and add value to Swedish or Nordic companies, is hugely important. This is an international business, but you need to be the local champion to be a global success and you need people with a global network and experience."

There's also no rivalry between venture capitalists in the region. HealthCap co-founder Björn Odlander welcomed the news that a new vc fund in the Nordics with a life science focus – Eir Ventures – was able to raise its first fund in 2020. For Odlander this illustrated the strength of the region's ecosystem, underlined by the fact that two of the founders at Eir have backgrounds in HealthCap and Novo Seeds.

Møller agrees that forming syndicates and working together with other vcs is an essential part of developing life science innovations into viable companies. They can share knowledge while acting independently:

> "We have a very good relationship with HealthCap where we both roll up our sleeves and split the tasks, share the knowledge and come to a conclusion."

According to Møller, the involvement of regional vcs is important in attracting international funding to companies as they grow.

> "Foreign investors, including vcs from the us, find comfort when they see that so-called local funds such as Novo Seeds or HealthCap are invested in the company, helping them focus the strategy and build the company, also navigating the landscape where innovation might have come out of northern European academic institutions," he explains.

Finding innovations to invest in can come from multiple sources. Sometimes vcs are approached directly by research scientists, other times ideas can come from discussing the portfolios of other vcs, and both Novo Seeds and HealthCap keep abreast of projects in universities or life science incubator hubs.

Novo Seeds also plays an important role in ensuring the continued support to the Nordic venture capital sector itself. As well as working with HealthCap as a collaboration partner, Novo Seeds invests in HealthCap's funds. Møller continues:

> "We have two relationships with them, we are a so-called lp in their fund, which means we also invest in HealthCap, because they are financially successful and a strong player in the Nordics who are good at picking ideas and companies in the life science sector to invest in. But then we also work with them as a professional venture syndication partner in our portfolio."

It All Starts With Good Science... but That's Just a Part of It

"WHAT MAKES THIS business so important and fun is that you must have optimism – otherwise it wouldn't work. You have to be able to see a need and think that there is a way of solving at least some of that need by using breakthroughs in science."

So says Eugen Steiner, an early member of the HealthCap team, when describing the journey of one of the VC's earliest investments. Back in 1997 HealthCap invested in the science of pyrosequencing, a method of DNA sequencing (determining the order of nucleotides in DNA) based on detecting light using the same biochemical reaction as that which causes fireflies to glow. Traditionally, DNA sequencing was done using a time-consuming process of degrading the DNA and analysing the different components. With pyrosequencing a light reaction is used to determine if the relevant components are present. The principle led to the first "next-generation sequencing" instrument and to a revolution in life science research.

DNA sequencing was becoming more and more important in scientific discovery but was also highly specialised and complex. Two tenacious and eminent Swedish scientists in the field – Mathias Uhlén and Pål Nyrén – persevered and in 1993 led a group that published a major breakthrough.

Uhlén recalls: "We applied for research funding several years following our discovery. The funders thought it was a great concept but told us they didn't really believe it would work and the funding was rejected!" However, HealthCap was convinced by the science and saw the opportunity to develop the innovation for use in other scientific discovery processes. It grabbed the chance to fund a company that could make this complex process become more accessible for use in scientific innovation. Uhlén continues: "We published the process in the top international journal *Science* in 1998, which really helped prove the scientific innovation, but HealthCap's support enabled the scientific idea to become a relied-upon process in lab work."

It was one of HealthCap's first investments and arguably one of the most scientifically advanced. HealthCap's ambition was to create a company to build and market an analytical instrument to carry out pyrosequencing, which would make DNA sequencing much more accessible to scientists.

Steiner explains: "DNA sequencing was becoming more and more important as it evolved, but it was a very specialised area and required very experienced scientists to oversee the process."

He continues: "It went from being complex scientific squiggles on paper lab reports to becoming the basis of a start-up. We had a clear vision of creating a lab-based machine that was simple, so that it didn't need to be run only by people with PhDs."

The company Pyrosequencing A/B was born with HealthCap funding and Steiner took on the role of CEO. He explains the advantages of having specialist investor backing:

> "I had run small companies before but the only external financing I knew was loans from the bank. Here we had the support of investors who understood the science, who could support us as we created a network of inventors, developers and others who could nurture and help develop the business."

As the first CEO of the company, Steiner's primary focus was to navigate the company through the early years before looking towards the public markets. Erik Walldén was brought in as the second CEO to execute the market launch of the technology, and he also presided over the company's IPO on the Swedish stock exchange where it raised around SEK 1 billion (at the time around USD 115 million).

"The IPO and market launch were the second transformational event in the company's history – with the first being the initial funding from HealthCap that nurtured its early development," said Steiner.

The scientific founder, Uhlén, also underlines the importance of the injection of VC funding. He states:

"Pyrosequencing – or Biotage, as it was renamed after one of the companies we acquired – would never have happened without HealthCap's support. It believed in us, put in a fantastic CEO and then helped navigate the company through the IPO, which by the way was one of the largest on the Swedish exchange at the time."

After the IPO the company invested heavily in the development of the science and in acquiring other companies to create a broader range of products to be used to improve lab processes and scientific discovery. In 2003 Pyrosequencing acquired the US company Biotage, adding purification and separation systems to the product range as well as giving the company a foothold in the all-important US market. Following the acquisition, the company changed its name to Biotage.

However, the growth of the company was also taking it in a different strategic direction. Steiner recalls:

"It started with great science. We had developed an amazing instrument that was simple to use and became an important piece of lab equipment. But over time, as the company grew and addressed the market, it had developed more into what I call a *shovel and tools* business. This required a different type of leadership as the selling process is completely different to that of a drug. So, in 2006 the Board of Directors brought in Torben Jørgensen as CEO, and he has made the business the success it is today."

Jørgensen describes himself as an industrialist, with a financial and commercial background. Having moved from his native Denmark to Stockholm in the early 2000s, he had experience of running two other biotech companies in Sweden – including one with HealthCap backing. Björn Odlander, HealthCap's managing partner, asked him to take over as CEO and the Board of Directors gave him a clear instruction that his goal was to make Biotage profitable. "The company had invested hugely, using the funds raised by the IPO, and was still making a loss. I took over in 2006 and within nine months we had turned a SEK 75 million loss into a SEK 6 million profit."

For Jørgensen, it also became clear that although pyrosequencing was a vital part of drug discovery, it was no longer a strategic fit in the type of business Biotage had become. He continues:

"I began looking at the right home for pyrosequencing. Initially we were talking to major players in the field about out-licensing. We were ready to sign such a deal with Qiagen, but at the last minute they came back to the table with an offer to buy the entire pyrosequencing business. It really was an excellent outcome, both for Qiagen and Biotage."

The deal gave Biotage the financial muscle to pursue other growth opportunities within the business, and under Jørgensen's watch the company delivered 25 per cent EBIT growth for 12 years in a row.

All good things come to an end though, and as the HealthCap fund invested in Biotage needed to close, the VC sold its stake in around 2008. For Jørgensen, who moved up to become chairman of the board of Biotage in 2019, it was also a logical step for HealthCap. He remembers:

"They were moving away from medtech and focusing their strategy more on investing in life science drug breakthroughs. But they can really take pride in what they created. They were strong supporters and went into it from 1997 to nurture a company based on a scientific breakthrough and an understanding of how to translate that into easily useable lab equipment."

Steiner admits the Pyrosequencing/Biotage investment probably wouldn't make the cut for HealthCap today due to the VC's current strategy:

"We are more focused on therapeutics, so we wouldn't invest in Biotage as it is today, even though it is a fantastic business. It is a good example of what needs to be done in supporting innovation financially, so we can use the science to create tools for the industry that can then be used in other scientific innovations. It's a fantastic story."

As well as being an eminent scientist, Uhlén has started around 20 life science companies. He believes that although some inventions can be nurtured in the academic environment for longer than others, you nearly always need outside funding in the end. In his view, HealthCap provided both funding to help develop his innovation and established a great workplace:

"I am so grateful to HealthCap as it would never have happened without their support. They are such an important driver of innovation in the life science industry. At Biotage the team at HealthCap were also integral in creating an atmosphere where we all worked very hard – but we also had a very good time. Of course, we had some disagreements, but we were able to really discuss the issues and ideas and then take decisions and move forward in the direction we had agreed on."

Uhlén is a seasoned entrepreneur in the field of life science. Even so, he points to Biotage as the company he is most proud of, both because of the original technology based on scientific innovation and the fact that the company has gone from strength to strength and it now has gone from start-up to unicorn status, which is when a company is worth more than a billion dollars. He recalls:

"I know I am biased but the pyrosequencing concept was absolutely fantastic, and it was very much pioneering at the time. I am also proud of the fact that the whole principle of next-generation sequencing has led to a change in the world and a large step forward in scientific understanding of human biology and disease."

He continues:

"From a more straightforward business side, I am also very impressed that we managed to build this instrument and raise so much money via an IPO to build the powerhouse of a company that still exists today. I am not actively part of the business any more, but I couldn't be prouder of it."

FACT
ART!

Finding the Sweet Spot in Life Science Investment

ONE OF THE first things you notice when visiting HealthCap's head office in Stockholm is a huge telescope, mounted on a tripod, standing in a corner. Björn Odlander bought the antique maritime telescope almost two decades ago, and today it stands as a symbol for HealthCap's focus on the long term and the need to understand what is happening in the distant future. He elaborates:

> "The telescope was originally used to enhance accuracy in coastal artillery attacks on enemy ships. Visitors to our offices often joke that we must be using it to spy on our competitors so we can outsmart them. But for me, it is more a symbol of how important it is to keep focus on the long term and to strive to understand as much as possible about how things look now and what might happen in the future. By doing that we can make better decisions here and now."

Just as the telescope once provided insight for more accurate attacks on the enemy, today partners at HealthCap gather as much information as possible to inform their due diligence process on life science innovations. Investing in early-stage life science companies is a venture in the true sense of the word. The potential pitfalls are many and there is a risk of failure. The rewards, though, are potentially high, with good levels of returns. By building on its longevity in the sector, HealthCap has created a focused strategy to try and mitigate some of the risks of failure while maximising the potential for success.

A core foundation for HealthCap's investment strategy is that successful venture capital investing is a mixture of both art and science. It believes the combination of the two disciplines creates the sweet spot that can lead to good returns and benefits to patients. In its view, life science venture capitalists need to navigate scientifically through a very complex universe and be able to understand and explain complex ideas and points of view to a broad group of people – skills often used in the arts. It takes time and experience to master the art of life science, with failures along the way inevitable and an important part of the learning process. HealthCap advisor the late Frank Caufield neatly summed it up: "This is the last apprenticeship business."

After 25 years of investing and working with more than 100 companies, HealthCap has gained valuable experience from investments that have worked and those which have not. One key learning is that to generate great returns you need to select opportunities with high potential. This means diligently assessing the risk–reward profile and ensuring that a return can be generated in a capital-efficient and timely manner. Although there is always an element of luck, both good and bad, in life science innovation, HealthCap's focused strategy attempts to minimise the risk of failure.

In the early years HealthCap's investment approach was relatively opportunistic, but as the team gained experience it was able to develop and refine the strategy to be more targeted. On top of navigating the science, HealthCap also had to meet the challenges presented by macro-economic events. During the early part of the millennium, when the entire venture capital industry was in distress, HealthCap used the opportunity to evaluate its investment strategy to find the right recipe for improved returns in the new landscape. By comparing successful investments with the less successful ones, it identified some common themes and formulated its strategy around the factors that the successful exits had in common. Over subsequent years the team regularly evaluated the strategy to ensure it continues to evolve in line with developments in both the life science sector and the macro-economic landscape.

HealthCap nowadays co-managing partner Mårten Steen explains:

> "We have a strategy that is targeted to leverage great science while maximising returns and our learnings from past experiences are important to identify the critical factors for a successful investment. At the same time we are aware of the macro environment and the constantly developing life science sector, and our strategic approach is flexible enough to take account of these factors."

Over the years HealthCap has gravitated more towards biotech and drug development because these investments have been more successful and generated better returns. The core focus of the VC's investment strategy is highly innovative therapies with breakthrough potential that can treat or cure patients suffering from severe diseases.

HealthCap partner Kristina Ekberg believes it is here that real and important differences can be made to benefit multiple stakeholders, including patients, doctors, investors, healthcare systems and society: "HealthCap's investments nurture scientific breakthroughs through the early stage where funding is scarce, so that life-saving treatments can be developed, creating value for both patients and payers, and addressing the issue of healthcare budget constraints."

HealthCap's refined investment strategy has also helped to attract a growing number of good-quality business proposals pitched to the team. It is clearer to others what HealthCap is looking for, and it is also easier for the HealthCap team to identify new opportunities that fit under the well-defined strategy.

One important criteria of HealthCap's investment strategy is to select companies that have the potential to bring their products to the market without a strategic partner. This allows more flexibility and autonomy for portfolio companies when setting strategy and allows them a range of strategic options as the company develops. Steen elaborates:

> "We really want to build companies which can control their destiny. Having independence, meaning you are not locked in to one party and you are not dependent on third-party decisions. You can then choose how to evolve the business and best create value. Having real autonomy is a powerful position to be in when negotiating with potential buyers and often results in better returns for the investor."

The search for companies that can control their destiny has driven HealthCap to focus more on niche indications, such as rare diseases and precision medicine. Learnings from successful ventures in these areas, such as Actelion, Jerini or Algeta, further validated this approach.

There are also other advantages in focusing on niche indications. Development timelines are shorter and clinical studies can be carried out with relatively fewer patients compared to trials for large disease indications, meaning results can be seen more quickly and development costs are lower. Success rates are also higher than in traditional pharma because these therapies are often very efficacious and addressing the root cause of disease, making a real difference in treatment outcome. Such precision medicines or treatments for rare diseases where there are no current alternatives can make a big difference to both patients and healthcare systems – something that is important to regulators when considering marketing approvals for drugs. By improving patient outcomes the burden on healthcare services, to provide other treatment regimens or long stays in hospital for patients, can also be reduced. Steen continues:

> "We've seen an increased focus from the pharmaceutical industry on precision medicine and rare disease over the last ten years or so. Today larger companies are looking for these kinds of assets, and as we moved relatively early into this field our portfolio companies are well positioned to offer products which "big pharma" companies are looking for to fill their pipelines. This gives our companies an even stronger ability to control their own destiny as there are multiple interested strategic partners to consider to partner or to agree a company acquisition. "

HealthCap believes in being an active partner and continuously working with business development. It does this by building strong relationships with strategic partners such as other investors and potential buyers and keeping them informed of the activities and projects of HealthCap portfolio companies, which makes it easier for all parties when considering future potential mergers, acquisitions or financings.

In order to reduce risk before investing, HealthCap has also developed an extensive due diligence process. The team methodically assesses the risk, evaluating what is known and proven, and whether additional critical work is needed before making an investment. HealthCap believes it is crucial to have a holistic view during the due diligence process, evaluating the scientific pedigree and the totality of the data to make sure that the science and data corroborate from all angles.

Odlander explains: "Understanding the underlying biology of a disease and the detailed mechanism of action of a proposed treatment is key to the fruitful development of a novel therapeutic that can contribute to the treatment of a devastating disease. This understanding is also essential to making a successful investment."

Another part of the due diligence process is to scrutinise the integrity and protection of the investment opportunity. HealthCap spends a lot of time evaluating competitiveness from different angles, including the competitive landscape and whether the product will have a clear differentiation in the marketplace, and has solid intellectual property protecting the product. At the end of a thorough due diligence process, HealthCap can understand and calculate the risk, and feel more comfortable that it is a risk worth taking.

Being an active investor is also about recognising the different needs of companies as they grow. HealthCap continuously evaluates the management teams of its portfolio companies to ensure they have the right entrepreneurial spirit and expertise for each part of the journey in building the company. For this, HealthCap's extensive network of experts, advisors, serial entrepreneurs and industry leaders is invaluable, providing a source for executive recruitment, additional skill sets and expert advice when needed.

Another aspect carefully monitored by HealthCap is to ensure fund resources are allocated optimally – in other words, making sure that good companies are resourced appropriately to build on success. Spotting and supporting the winners is critical for a VC fund, because it is the big wins that really drive overall fund performance. The key for HealthCap is to regularly assess the performance of its portfolio, to make sure it is invested in the right companies at the right time. This process is known as dynamic asset allocation, and it allows the team to identify when it is appropriate to access other sources of capital such as non-dilutive financing or by raising additional equity from investors. One of the golden rules in venture capital is to take money when it is offered – but there is a constant debate about when is the right time to open up for other investors and whether a portfolio company can be brought to the next inflection point without new investors, which avoids dilution of HealthCap's investment. Dynamic asset allocation also allows HealthCap to identify early on which companies underperform, so that losses can be reduced and resources can be channelled to follow the winners.

Over the last 25 years HealthCap has evolved an investment strategy and method that has brought success. Something Steen believes provides a solid foundation for the future: "Of course, the dynamics of the market can be bumpy over time, but ultimately, the current pace of innovation is unprecedented and we believe this will continue. New technologies continuously emerge that allow us to tackle diseases that have not been possible to address before."

He continues:

> "We firmly believe that the era of precision medicine has just begun. By having this as the focus of our investment strategy, we try to ensure we work with the right medicine for the right patient. HealthCap's strength is that we continue to learn from and build on our experiences – and stay disciplined. We feel privileged that our investors have given us the confidence to take this journey and are excited about the road ahead of us."

CONCLUSION:

A Golden Age of Medical Research

WE ARE LIVING in a golden age of medical research thanks to our ever-increasing understanding of cell chemistry.

"If I have seen further it is by standing on the shoulders of giants." When Sir Isaac Newton made this remark in a letter in 1675, he meant that his discoveries in the field of optics – such as determining that the visible light spectrum is made up of all seven colours of the rainbow – would never have happened if it had not been for the insights he had gained from his predecessors.

The metaphor of "standing on the shoulders of giants" can be traced back to the 12th century, and it is often used to describe the way a discovery always builds on the foundation of previous research. However, we need to modify the expression to characterise the explosive growth in knowledge that is currently occurring in medicine. We no longer stand on the shoulders of just a few giants but on a global network of researchers who have often dedicated their lives to science. Thousands upon thousands of people have refined the tools we use today to study the smallest component of life: the cell. By using genomics, proteomics, transcriptomics and other "-omics" techniques we can now generate an image of complex cellular machinery within the space of a couple of months. In much the same way as children doing a "spot the differences" puzzle, scientists can compare diseased and healthy cells to figure out what has gone wrong in diseased cells. Understanding that is a crucial first step in developing pharmaceuticals.

Things were very different in the early 1960s when I began my scientific career. The scientists whose shoulders I stood on were Kurzrok, Lieb, Goldblatt and von Euler. In the 1930s, they discovered a component of semen that caused muscles to contract. Three decades later, Sune Bergström, Jan Sjövall and I, along with our colleagues at the Karolinska Institutet, succeeded in purifying these substances – prostaglandin E1 and E2 – and determining their chemical structures. Insights into the structure of prostaglandins helped us to understand how they are formed in the body. Then one discovery led to another, and it became clear that we had discovered an entirely new molecular system within the cell. Through this system a number of signalling molecules known as eicosanoids are formed. Eicosanoids affect everything from blood pressure and the immune response to muscle contraction and pain perception.

Findings from our analysis of this system enabled John Vane and his colleagues to discover how acetylsalicylic acid can reduce inflammation in the body and that low doses of acetylsalicylic acid can prevent heart attacks. Research into eicosanoids has also contributed to drug treatments for allergies, high blood pressure and glaucoma. A synthetic analogue of prostaglandin E2 is used to induce labour for childbirth.

So basic scientific research, sparked by curiosity, has given millions of people healthier lives and helped thousands of children into the world. But we had no expectations that our work would lead to those results when we began. To us it was a pleasant surprise that the molecular system that had attracted our interest turned out to play so many key roles in the body.

Many 20th-century medical advances came about in a similar way. Scientists who started pulling at an interesting thread could arrive at sudden, unexpected findings, and quite a few discoveries arose through a bit of luck. One familiar example happened when Alexander Fleming inadvertently left some culture plates containing staphylococcus bacteria out on his lab bench when he went away on holiday. When he returned and was about to throw the plates away, he noticed that mould had started to grow on one of them and that the bacterial colonies immediately surrounding the mould had been killed off.

Many people would have given this observation no further thought, but Fleming had been searching for an effective antibacterial substance. From that mould he was able to purify penicillin, one of the most beneficial medicines to humanity.

However, relying on chance and good fortune in pharmaceutical research is hardly a sustainable approach. That became especially apparent in the 1990s, when the number of new medicines began to dwindle. Few new pharmaceuticals were approved, and many of the ones that did make it to market merely aped existing therapies. Nearly every pharmaceutical company produced its own version of cholesterol-reducing statins or SSRIs (Selective Serotonin Reuptake Inhibitors) for treating depression. Little innovation was happening, and it was a costly endeavour to prove that a new variation was superior to existing pharmaceuticals. Huge studies were needed to establish wafer-thin statistical advantages, and that was enormously expensive.

While pharmaceutical companies were going through a crisis in the 1990s, we scientists were experiencing a revolution in the techniques available to study cells. Tools for gene cloning and DNA sequencing underwent continual improvements. In 1990 the Human Genome Project was launched with the aim of mapping the entire human genetic sequence, which consists of approximately 3.2 billion nucleotides. The scope of this project was on a par with the moon landings. As more chunks of the genetic code were revealed, our understanding of the causes of various diseases increased.

We also acquired new and more powerful ways to study proteins, the functional molecules within cells. Using monoclonal antibodies, fluorescent markers and advanced microscopy methods, suddenly we could follow the path of proteins within cells and generate a detailed picture of their structure. For example, an understanding of the structure of receptors – the proteins that sit on a cell's surface and transmit signals into the cell – is fundamental in the development of many medicines.

It's also worth mentioning the unexpected discoveries that have been made within the field of RNA. This molecular relative of DNA was long assumed to have a relatively passive role in the cell. However, in the late 1990s RNA was shown to be capable of regulating gene activity via a mechanism called RNA interference. That insight sparked greater interest in RNA and has led to new ideas for pharmaceutical formulations.

Last but not least, techniques to synthesise molecules that can serve as medicines have been streamlined and scaled up. Increasing numbers of pharmaceuticals are based on proteins, particularly antibodies. Their function can be optimised by means of artificial evolution. For example, several of HealthCap's portfolio companies – Nordic Nanovector, SynOx Therapeutics, Adcendo, Precirix and Fusion Pharmaceuticals – employ specially designed antibodies that act like targeted missiles to seek out malignant tumours and direct treatments to them.

This is just a small sample of the progress that has been made in molecular biology since I began my scientific career. Experiments we once could only have dreamed of doing have become routine in laboratories around the world. Questions that might have taken decades to answer can now be solved in just few days.

This has been a huge leap forward, which is starting to bear fruit in the pharmaceutical field as well. If 20th-century medical advances often depended on chance occurrences, 21st-century medical science is more rational. Nowadays a researcher can set out to develop a treatment for a particular genetic disorder, for example, and achieve that goal. It takes knowledge, determination and expertise, but there is far less need for strokes of luck like Fleming's forgotten culture plates.

One should always be cautious when assessing the present day, but there are many signs that medical research is in the midst of a golden era. Progress in developing new medicines, vaccines and diagnostic techniques has accelerated. In the early 1990s, the US Food & Drug Administration approved around 25 new medicines per year, of which only half were regarded as significantly beneficial to patients. The rest provided little added value. Compare that with the last four years, 2018–2021, when the average number of new medicines approved was more than 50 annually, many of which help against diseases and disorders that used to be untreatable.

One group of patients who have benefited from life-changing new treatments are people with autoimmune conditions. People diagnosed in the 1990s with rheumatoid arthritis, psoriasis, lupus or multiple sclerosis often faced a painful future as their immune system gradually attacked their own body. But through detailed study of the signalling pathways that control the immune system, scientists have developed targeted treatments that halt the destructive progress of these conditions.

Meanwhile, recent cancer research has focused on unleashing the power of immune cells and targeting them at tumours. Thanks to Nobel Prize-winning immunotherapies, it's now even possible to cure metastasised cancers – something that was previously impossible. The number of treatments in this field, including some from HealthCap's companies Targovax, Priothera and Carisma Therapeutics, is growing rapidly. In 2020 alone, immunotherapies for treating around 20 types of cancer received approval.

The number of treatments for rare genetic disorders is also increasing steadily. This used to be an unprofitable area that few pharmaceutical companies were willing to invest in. Trying to find the cause of a genetic disorder was like looking for a needle in a whole field of haystacks. It could take years. But with so many new molecular biology tools available to us, we can identify a missing gene within the space of a few weeks. Then it takes a few years to understand how the mutation affects the body and another few years to develop a candidate treatment.

We are also getting closer to realising our dream of being able to cure genetic disorders. Vivet Therapeutics and Ultragenyx Inc., two companies backed by HealthCap, are working on gene therapies for inherited liver disorders. They aim to use modified viruses to introduce therapeutic genes into the body.

While medical science is making such huge strides right now, there are still many challenges. For example, many of the new life-saving cancer treatments can have serious side effects. So the targeted treatments we already have need to become even more precise. Another major challenge is finding treatments for multifactorial illnesses – disorders driven by complex mechanisms. But one thing is certain: the more we learn about the body and its mechanisms, the better we will become at solving these problems.

One of the giants whose shoulders Newton had in mind was the recipient of his letter, Robert Hooke. Hooke was one of the first scientists to observe microorganisms under a microscope. He coined the term "cell" in 1665. Newton himself did not make much use of microscopes, which were in their infancy at that time, but he predicted that if they became powerful enough to enlarge objects to 3,000 or 4,000 times their actual size, it would be possible to see atoms.

That must have been an astounding concept at the time. It's equally astounding today to imagine what will happen when 3D printers become capable of printing entire organs. Or when cross-pollination between molecular biology, supercomputers and AI progresses to the point where the body's entire biochemistry can be simulated on a computer. Anyone who wants to retain their credibility should avoid speculating about the future. The only thing we know for certain is that when generations of scientists stand on each other's shoulders, the results can often surpass our wildest imagination. And if firms like HealthCap continue to fund research to achieve scientists' visions, we will all benefit.

Bengt Samuelsson, MD, PhD

WHAT'S
NEXT?

TRYGG

HealthCap So Far

>€1.2Bn Funds raised from >100 institutional investors	**€400Mn** Annual R&D budget in active companies
30 Approved drugs	**>50** Approved healthtech products
46 IPOs	**96** Exits

126	**€56Bn**
Funded companies	Accumulated company value
~40	**~3Mn**
Average number of ongoing clinical trials the last ten years	Treated patients
>50K	**12**
Direct and indirect jobs created	Unicorns created

What's Next? – to be Continued

Funds raised	Annual R&D Budget in active companies
Approved drugs	Approved healthtech products
IPOs	Exits

Funded companies	Accumulated company value
Average number of ongoing clinical trials	Treated patients
Direct and indirect jobs created	Unicorns created

VALUATION
HealthCap IV, L.P.
LIVET
WORK
HARD
&
BE NICE
TO PEOPLE

HealthCap IV
HealthCap IV KB
HealthCap IV Bis, L.P.
HealthCap V
HealthCap V, L.P.
SVCA

4
9
5
8
2
7
1
3
10
6

Stockholm office:
1. Per Samuelsson, 2. Johan Christenson, 3. Sofie Wennerqvist,
4. Alex Valcu, 5. Carl Kilander, 6. Staffan Lindstrand, 7. Jakob Regberg,
8. Georg Beiske, 9. Gunilla Byström, 10. Björn Odlander, 11. Anki Forsberg,
12. Per Olof Eriksson, 13. Mårten Steen, 14. Carl-Johan Dalsgaard,
15. Kristina Ekberg, 16. Eugen Steiner, 17. Mikael Grundström,
18. Fanny Fredriksson, 19. Marile Schiess, 20. Emma Blomqvist.

ROBERT
BROBERG
HÄNDER

Lausanne office:
1. Gunilla Bosshard, 2. Fabrice Bernhard, 3. Dag Richter.

Index

Text: Rachel Curtis Gravesen
Text: Ann Fernholm, pages 137–141
Translation: Ruth Urbom, pages 137–141
Paintings: Jesper Waldersten
Photos: Erik G. Svensson page 145, Dan Coleman pages 150–151,
David Serkin page 154
Design: Patric Leo
Layout: Amelie Stenbeck Ramel
Editor: Christopher Westhorp
Editorial advisory board: Malena Bergroth,
Björn Odlander, Annica Triberg, Jeppe Wikström
Colour adjustement: Marcus Erixson
Pre-press: Italgraf Media
Print: Graphicom, Italy, 2022
ISBN 978-91-7126-544-9

www.healthcap.eu
www.maxstrom.se